John Matthews

A Voyage to the River Sierra-Leone on the Coast of Africa

John Matthews

A Voyage to the River Sierra-Leone on the Coast of Africa

ISBN/EAN: 9783337816551

Printed in Europe, USA, Canada, Australia, Japan

Cover: Foto ©Andreas Hilbeck / pixelio.de

More available books at **www.hansebooks.com**

A

VOYAGE

TO

THE RIVER SIERRA-LEONE,

ON

THE COAST OF AFRICA;

CONTAINING AN ACCOUNT OF THE.

TRADE AND PRODUCTIONS OF THE COUNTRY,

AND OF THE

CIVIL AND RELIGIOUS CUSTOMS AND MANNERS
OF THE PEOPLE;

IN A SERIES OF LETTERS

TO A FRIEND IN ENGLAND.

By JOHN MATTHEWS,
Lieutenant in the Royal Navy;

DURING HIS RESIDENCE IN THAT COUNTRY
IN THE YEARS 1785, 1786, AND 1787.

WITH

AN ADDITIONAL LETTER
ON THE SUBJECT OF
THE AFRICAN SLAVE TRADE.

ALSO,

A CHART OF PART OF THE COAST OF AFRICA, FROM
CAPE ST. ANN, TO THE RIVER RIONOONAS; WITH
A VIEW OF THE ISLAND BANANAS.

LONDON:

PRINTED FOR B. WHITE AND SON, AT HORACE'S HEAD
FLEET-STREET; AND J. SEWELL, CORNHILL. 1788.

CONTENTS.

LETTER

LETTER I.

Sierra-Leone, Sept. 25, 1785.

MY DEAR FRIEND,

I EMBRACE the firſt opportunity to inform you of my ſafe arrival at the place of
my deſtination, after an agreeable paſſage
of thirty days, in which nothing happened ſufficiently intereſting to communicate.
In paſſing between the Grand Canary and Te-
neriffe we were fortunate in having ſuch a
view of the *Peak* as is ſeldom ſeen.

The top, then covered with ſnow, appeared far above the clouds in the pure
regions of ether; and, from its extreme ſum-

B   mit,

mit, iffued a bright flame. Round the bafe of the mountain, but above the culti-vated country, the clouds gathered in thick darknefs, frcm whence iffued ftorms, thunder, and lightening, upon the plains below.

Your letter of the 20th of March did not reach me before my departure from Liverpool, as I failed on the 22d, or I fhould have fully explained to you my motives for going abroad.

There is fuch a contraft, you obferve, between the glory of naval victories and the lifelefs fcenes of commercial purfuits, that it muft be difficult to reconcile the mind to the fudden tranfition. I confefs it is true, but it will be fufficient for the prefent, at once to obferve, that, after ferving as a lieutenant during the whole of the late war in the Weft Indies, and fharing in almoft every action during that period, I found myfelf, at the peace, under a necef-

fity

fity of exerting myfelf fome way or other, to fupport that appearance in life which might not be unworthy a Britifh naval officer. In a commercial country like ours, in which the character of a merchant is as refpectable and as ufeful an one as any in the ftate, I am free to own, it was with much pleafure i turned my thoughts to trade. I had indeed an additional inducement to connect myfelf with gentlemen who traded to the coaft of Africa, becaufe, having before been engaged in that commerce, I thought myfelf more competent to undertake a fimilar employment.

I have juft finifhed my negociations with the natives for a convenient fituation to erect ftores and workmen's houfes. The fame place was purchafed by a former agent to the fame company by which I am employed, whom the natives murdered in a moft horrid manner ince which time

B 2 (about

(about fourteen years ago) *not a white man has dared to put his foot on shore:* and, prior to that period, they had deſtroyed the crews of ſeveral veſſels, and plundered their cargoes. It was with ſome difficulty I could prevail on the natives who reſided in the bay to meet me; they were apprehenſive I ſhould take vengeance upon them for their former cruelty, a ſentiment congenial to their diſpoſition; as they imagine it indicates cowardice and want of ſpirit to let the enemy eſcape when an opportunity of revenge preſents itſelf. I however took every means to inſpire them with confidence, and ſo far ſucceeded, that I convened an aſſembly of the king and neighbouring chiefs, and of all the inhabitants of every denomination. Image to yourſelf the ſhore of a little ſandy bay covered with black men, women, and children. Under the ſhade of a tree ſat the king in an arm-chair, dreſſed in a ſuit of blue ſilk,

trimmed

trimmed with silver lace, with a laced hat and ruffled shirt, and shoes and stockings. On each side sat his principal people, and behind him two or three of his wives.

I began by informing them that all past acts should be buried in oblivion; that, notwithstanding the very bad character they had, I hoped the consequences of their former crimes, which they had severely felt in the loss of their trade, would, in future, make them behave better. I pointed out to them the condition which those men had fallen into who had been the chief promoters of their former cruelties; that though they got immense spoil, yet nothing now remained of it; and that they were punished and despised both by God and man. I stated to them that, by their own laws, they were bound to protect the stranger from insult and oppression; and that all white men were strangers in their land: and although the place we were

then

then fitting upon was the property of my employers, yet, to avoid a retrofpect of the paft, I would again purchafe it. I expatiated pretty largely on the power I was capable of exerting, fhould they attempt to deftroy my property or people; but that I wifhed to live in peace and amity; and gave them the ftrongeft affurances that they might at all times rely upon my word. That if ever they fou: i me guilty of an untruth, I would forfeit every claim to their confidence; and concluded by making a hole in the ground, and faying in this grave I bury all paft animofities, whoever opens it fhall be fubject to a *palaver*, *Ya, ob', ya, ob'fafeé*, (a term of approbation) refounded from every quarter, and echoed from the furrounding hills. The king and myfelf filled up the hole, which ceremony put an end to our affembly.

In the evening they brought an old man to me bound, and much bruifed with the

blows

blows he had received about the head and face: I inquired for what reason they brought him to me? they answered "The king ordered us to offer him to you provided you will promise never to suffer him to return on shore. It is this man who has bewitched us, and who is the cause of all the injury we have formerly done to white men; if you do not take him he cannot be permitted to return to land."—I declined the present for various reasons; but had I conceived the least idea of the intended fate of the poor unhappy victim, I should have considered it as a most fortunate event in my life, in preserving him from the horrid cruelty of his superstitious countrymen.

The canoe in which they brought the man put off from my vessel, and hovered in the bay till the sun was set; they then tied a stone to the neck of the unfortunate wretch and plunged him into the sea, where, in all probability, *he, in a few moments,*

B 4

ments, found a living fepulchre in the bowels of a fhark, which abound very much in the river of Sierra-Leone.

I fhall conclude this letter with an affurance, that I fhall not be unmindful of my promife to tranfmit you fuch information concerning the cuftoms and particular ceremonies of the natives of the country, and the nature of the African trade, as I can collect from my own obfervations, or upon fuch authority as I can depend.

I am,

Dear Sir, &c.

LETTER II.

MY DEAR FRIEND,

THOUGH I have not hitherto had it in my power to collect much information concerning the manners, cuftoms, &c. of the natives of this country, yet, fuch as I am enabled to give you, I fhall from time to time take real pleafure in defcribing, as it is the only means I have *now* in my power of teftifying my friendfhip and efteem.

That you may the better underftand any future accounts I may fend you, I think it firft neceffary to give you a fhort geographical defcription of the country in general; I mean fuch an extent of it only to which our connexions in trade reach, with a map of the fea coaft, pointing out the outlines of

the

the coaſt and the principal rivers, and ſituations of the iſlands contiguous to the continent.

The ſea coaſt from the river Rionoonas,
which is the northern boundary to Cape St.
Ann, and which makes the ſouth ſide of the
bay of Sherbro', is an extent of ſixty-five
leagues, ſtretching nearly noith and ſouth,
and is indented with many rivers and
creeks; ſeveral of which are navigable for
veſſels of burthen, and all of them for ſmall
craft.

The river Rionoonas is very broad, and
rapid at its entrance into the ſea. Its preſent name, as well as the names of moſt
of the other rivers, owe their origin to the
Portugueſe, who formed very extenſive ſet-
tlements ſoon after their diſcovery of Africa. -
Part of their deſcendants remained here ſo
late as the beginning of the preſent century;
and veſtiges of their fort, and ſome other
buildings, are ſtill to be ſeen about thirty-
five

five miles up the river. The tradition of the country says the Portuguefe were driven from their fettlements on this river, for having frequently endeavoured to fub- jugate the ftates round them; and to make all the natives without diftinction their flaves, by bridling the country with forts; a mea- fure which they have fully carried into effect at their principal fettlement of Baf- fou, near Gambia. This river was former- ly a place of great trade for flaves and ivory, but the flave merchants now take a different route. Ivory is ftill purchafed in confiderable quantities. — The natives are called Nalloes, and are very ingenious in fabricating cotton cloths, which they fell to their more fouthern neighbours.—The fea- coaft of this country is every where, till you reach Sierra-Leone, low; and in moft parts fwampy and interfected with creeks, which generally connect the adjoining rivers, and form an excellent inland navigation.

At

At unequal diſtances from five to twenty miles, in a right line from the ſea, the country riſes gradually, and beyond that diſtance, in many places, towers into high hills and lofty mountains, which, after a tornado, when the air is pure, may be ſeen twenty or twenty-five leagues at ſea.

From Rionoonas to the Cappatches is about five leagues ſouth eaſt: this river is broad and deep within, but the entrances are all ſhallow, formed by little iſlands, ſimilar to the mouths of the Ganges. The inhabitants are called Bagoes, and are very induſtrious in planting rice, making cloths, ſalt, and in fiſhing, and trading for ivory; they alſo raiſe vaſt quantities of poultry.

From Cappatches to Cape Verges, which is a low point ſtretching out into the ſea, is S.S.E. two leagues; from thence to the river Riopongeos, which is S.S.E. five leagues. The coaſt is formed of a number of ſmall iſlands called Caxa Iſlands—the
inhabitants

inhabitants are Nalloes and Bagoes, and employ themfelves in a fimilar manner to thofe I have juft defcribed.

The river Riopongeos, though not equal to the Rionoonas in fize, is yet one of the principal rivers for trade in this part of Africa; and, like the latter, has many large extenfive branches, where European and native traders are fettled. And it is worthy of remark, that the fame black merchants who vifit Gambia come likewife to this place.

The natives are originally Suzeés, but the principal people call themfelves Portuguefe, claiming their defcent from the colonifts of that nation who were formerly fettled here, though they do not retain the fmalleft trace of European extraction; but having had a white man once in the family, is fufficient to give them the appellation. They alfo profefs the Roman Catholic religion; and are vifited once or twice a year

by

by a prieſt from the Portugueſe ſettlement
at Baſſoo, who baptizes their children, and
receives their confeſſion of faith according
to his dictates; yet the moſt enlightened of
them are merely nominal Chriſtians. Their
religion principally conſiſts in repeating a
Pater Noſter, or an *Ave Maria*, and in wearing a large ſtring of beads round their neck,
with a croſs, or crucifix, ſuſpended. In
every other reſpect they follow the cuſtoms
and ceremonies of their pagan countrymen;
but generally exceed them in treachery and
revenge. The black merchants who bring
ſlaves and ivory down to this river, and the
adjoining one of Dembia, bring alſo large
herds of cattle, goats, and ſheep, which
form an article of traffic with the neighbouring countries. The natives are alſo induſtrious in cultivating rice, and in making
an inferior kind of cloth, mats, and ſalt.

From the Riopongeos to Dembia river is
ſouth-eaſt about eight leagues, where there is
a conſiderable

a confiderable trade; the natives are called Coobé Bagoes, which is only a difcriminating appellation, fimilar to our counties. From thence to Dania river is fouth-eaft four or five miles, where there is at prefent little trade; the inhabitants are Bagoes, and, like their neighbours at Dembia and the Riopongeos, are induftrious in fifhing, in cultivating rice, and making coarfe cloths, mats, and falt. From Dania the land juts out fouth-weft fix or feven miles to Tomba Point. Weft from Tomba about three miles lie the Ifles de Lofs, which are feven in number, three of which only are inhabited, the reft are little more than rocks, on the moft eaftern of which are our town and factory. Thefe iflands, by being detached from the main, are extremely pleafant, and in general healthy; the largeft, which is the weftern-moft, is almoft femicircular, rifing on both fides from the fea by a gentle afcent to a moderate height, covered with good timber trees;

trees; and furrounded on all fides, except to the north-eaft, by a rocky fhore. The factory ifland lies almoft north and fouth, with a high wood-crown'd hill at each end; which when firft feen from fea, makes it appear like two iflands. The road for fhipping is on the eaft fide; and, during the dry feafon, is extremely fafe, and pleafant; but in the tornado and rainy feafon there is no fecurity except in the goodnefs of your anchors and cables. The iflands are called by the natives Forotimá, which fignifies White Man's Land; and were not inhabited forty years ago, except by one fingle Bagoe family; but are now overftocked with a mixture of Bagoes, run away Suzee, and Mandingo flaves.

To the fouthward of Tomba the land recedes to the eaftward, and forms a deep bay between it, and a point called Matacong, which lies fouth-eaft eight leagues from the Ifles de Lofs. In the bottom of this bay are

the

rivers Quia, Porte, and Burria; the former
is a very confiderable place of trade, and has
many large towns on the different branches
of the river, in moſt of which are feveral
European refidents.   The chief trade of
the latter is rice.—The natives are Suzeés,
induſtrious in cultivating rice, and affiduous
in trade.

To the fouthward of Matacong runs Kiffey river, which is large and deep, into
which two other rivers empty themfelves
from Bierrareé and Kiangefa, which, as well
as Kiffey, are confiderable places of trade,
and the chief towns of the Mandingoes.—
Sama river lies two leagues to the fouthward of Kiffey, and is alfo a place of trade,
having feveral confiderable towns upon its
banks.—About fix leagues fouth of Sama
are the great and little Scarcies rivers, between which and Kiffey river is the Mandingo country: the natives are Mahomedans,
and as zealous promoters of their religion

C   as

as even Mahomed himfelf could wish.——
They cultivate great quantities of rice, but
are too lazy and too proud to attend to
trade, except when in want of what cannot
be acquired without it. The Scarcies are both
rivers of great trade for flaves, rice, and
camwood, and for the fruit colá, which
they fell to the Portuguefe traders from
Baffou.

The natives on the lower parts of the
river, and between it and Sierra-Leone, are
Bullams; but higher up, and on the north
fide, are Timmanies.——The ravages of time,
and the encroachments of the ocean are no
where more ftrongly marked than along
this coaft. Off the mouth of the Scarcies
river were many cohfiderable iflands nearly
adjoining to the continent, well remembered
by feveral old men now living, which are
now entirely overflowed by the fea, and
form a fand bank to the diftance of three or
four miles from the fhore, upon which
there

there is about two fathom water. The bank which is called the middle ground in Sierra-Leone river was, by the tradition of the natives, formerly joined to the Bullam fhore; and I had myfelf an opportunity of obferving that, in one rainy feafon, near a quarter of a mile of the weft end of the north-weft Turtle ifland, in the bay of Sherbro', was wafhed away, and that the ifland increafed by an accumulation of fand in an equal or greater proportion at the other end: the natives informed me this was the cafe with all the reft. Indeed it appears to me that they were originally not only all joined in one, but that they alfo were united with the neighbouring ifland of St. Ann; and, that thus united, they projected ten leagues from the prefent fhore.

It is, however, highly probable that their feparation has been occafioned by the impetuofity and inceffant attack of the waves

of the great weſtern ocean, urged forward
by the trade wind upon a flat ſhore. .

The moſt extraordinary circumſtance of
this kind is at the river Gallienas.—The
Portugueſe had formerly a colony there, and
erected a fort at the entrance of the river.
The ſpot on which the fort ſtood has now
ſeven fathom water over it, and is diſtant
ſix miles from the ſhore, to which the water
ſhoals gradually. Ships frequently loſe their
anchors upon it, or bring up fragments of
the old walls.

From the Scarcies to Sierra-Leone river is
ſouth three leagues. This noble river is at
leaſt two leagues wide at its entrance, and
has a ſafe and deep channel for ſhips of any
burthen, and affords, excellent anchorage
at all ſeaſons. It continues nearly the ſame
breadth for ſix or ſeven miles, and then
divides into two branches; one of which
contains Bance iſland, and runs to two
principal places of trade for ſlaves and
camwood,

camwood, called Rokelle and Port Logo; -
the other branch is called Bunch river, in
which is Gambia ifland, where the French
have a fort and factory. — On the north
fide of Sierra-Leone river the land is low
and level, and produces great quantities of
rice; the cultivation of which, and the
making of falt, are the chief occupations
of the natives, who, on both fides, are called
Bullams; but on the fouth fide it rifes into ,
hills, which, forming one upon the other,
towers into lofty mountains crowned with
perpetual verdure.—From the foot of thefe
hills points of land project into the fea, which
form excellent bays for fhipping and craft, and
convenient places for hauling the feine.—
The vallies near the fea are inhabited; but
few or any of the natives refide in the
interior part of the mountainous country;
which, if properly cleared and cultivated,
would, in my opinion, be equal in falubrity,
and fuperior in productions, to any of the

Well

Weft India iflands.—In coming in from
the fea in the dry feafon few profpects can
exceed the entrance into Sierra-Leone river.
Before you is the high land of Sierra-
Leone rifing from the Cape with the moft
apparent gentle afcent. Perpetual verdure
reigns over the whole extent, and the va-
riegated foliage of the different trees, with
the fhades caufed by the projecting hills
and unequal fummits, add greatly to the
beauty of the fcene.

The flopes of the leffer hills have the appearance of a high degree of cultivation, arifing
from the tracts of land, which had been
cultivated for two or three preceding years,
but were now covered with thick underwood
and rank weeds, that, at a diftance, give it the
appearance of pafture or pleafure grounds;
particularly as large fingle trees, for which
the natives have a veneration, are left
ftanding in different places, while the
newly

newly cleared ground has the appearance of ftubble or ploughed land.

Between the two capes, which are diftin-guifhed by their projection into the fea, and by fome remarkable trees, is a fine femi-circular bay, with a white fandy beach, edged with a beautiful grove of palms.— To the right is a diftant view of the Bana-na's ifle, and on the left is the Bullam fhore, fkirted with a white fandy beach, and decorated with clumps of palms and lofty trees. Several red cliffs are alfo dif-covered which ferve to break the line of uniformity; while, higher up the river, as far as the eye can reach, the trees feem to float upon the waving furface of the water; or, to a lively imagination, may appear like a fleet of fhips.

The natives at and about Sierra-Leone are not remarkable for their induftry or their honefty; they cultivate little more rice than is neceffary for their own con-

C 4   fumption

fumption from feafon to feafon; and, fhould a crop fail, they are frequently reduced to great diftrefs. Immoderately fond of liquor they part with every thing they are poffeffed of to acquire it; and when thofe means fail they purfue the fame which idle drunkards do in every part of the world, rob and plunder their neighbours; for few apply themfelves to trade.

From Cape Sierra-Leone to Falfe Cape is fouth two leagues; from thence to the pleafant ifland of Banana's is fouth fix leagues; you then enter the great bay of Sherbro', which is formed by Cape Shelling and Cape St. Ann. Several large rivers empty themfelves into this bay, which are marked in the chart, and which are places of great trade for flaves, camwood, and rice. The natives throughout Sherbro', as well as in the iflands, are called Bullams, and are in- duftrious in trade and agriculture; and par- ticularly famous for a manufactory of mat-

ting,

ting, extremely beautiful, and made of
ftained grafs.

The Turtle iflands are fituated on the
fouth fide, and the Plantains on the north
fide of this bay, and were formerly the refidence of eminent white and native traders.
Having conducted you fo far I fhall clofe
this long epiftle,

And am,

With the utmoft efteem,

Yours, &c. &c.

LETTER III.

Sierra-Leone, June 10, 1786.

DEAR SIR,

IN my laſt I gave you a deſcription of the ſea coaſt of this country, pointing out to you the names of the different nations who inhabit it; I ſhall in this deſcribe to you the climate and ſeaſons.

Cape St. Ann lies in latitude 7° 12′ north; Cape Sierra-Leone in 8° 12″ north; the Ifles de Loſs in 9° 20″; and the river Rio-noonas 10° 21′, and about 12 degrees or 48 minutes difference in time to the weſt-ward of London.—An abſtract from my journal for the years 1785 and 1786 will, I conceive, give you a more complete idea of

the

the feafons and temperature of the clime than I could otherwife convey,

January.—About the middle of this month we had three or four days rainy weather, blowing hard from the fouth-weft, with thunder and lightning.—The reft of the month moderate and variable, land and fea breezes, with pleafant weather; thermometer in the fhade; morning 75°, noon 85°, evening 80°, but expofed to the meridian fun from 90° to 100.

February.—Tolerable pleafant weather the whole of this month, with almoft conftant and regular fea and land breezes; the latter commencing about three in the morning and ending about ten, or fhifting round to the north-weft, which in the courfe of the day veered to the weft or fouth-weft. At this feafon the evenings and mornings are extremely pleafant; but it is very unwholefome to be out long after the fun is fet or before it has rifen, the dews being exceedingly

exceedingly copious and penetrating. The thermometer generally at the fame height as in the laft month.

March.—The firft of this month it rained very hard, with light foutherly and variable winds; the two following days had a ftrong land wind and thick fog, attended with a dry fharp air. It continued heavy weather from the horizon about 20° upwards, and clear and bright in the zenith the remainder of the month, with moderate land and fea breezes from north-weft to weft and fouth-weft; thermometer during the day in the fhade from 80° to 90°.

April.—Some rain about the middle of this month, with clofe cloudy weather and foutherly wind; the middle and latter parts clear and pleafant; the mornings generally calm, or light airs from the north-weft, which veered to the weft or fouth-weft in the evening; thermometer in the fhade from 80° to 86°.

May.

May.—Heavy rain the firſt three nights of this month; all the remainder fair and clear, with regular ſea breezes from north-weſt to ſouth-weſt every day. Cloſe in ſhore, and in the little bays light airs are felt off the land from midnight till nine or ten next morning. Thermometer in the ſhade as before, expoſed 95° to 100°.

June.—The beginning of this month fair and pleaſant weather: about the 8th it began to blow and rain from the north-ward; on the 13th had the firſt tornado; the remainder of the month frequent and heavy rain and ſoutherly wind from ſouth-eaſt to ſouth-weſt. The air raw, moiſt, and cold; the thermometer frequently falling to 72°, and on the ſun's breaking out riſing to 85° and 90°.

July.—During the whole of this month frequent and heavy rain, thunder and light-ning, and violent tornados; the wind vari-able,

able, but chiefly from the northward; frequently b!   ing hard for two or three days
together from the north-weſt. Thermometer variable as in laſt month.

Auguſt. — Much rain, but chiefly from
evening till morning, with ſtrong ſoutherly
winds all this month, and dark diſagreeable
weather. Thermometer generally high,
from 80° to 90°.

September.—Frequent ſhowers, but little
heavy rain during this month. In the firſt
part the wind was light and va ⁿt'⁻ with
frequent calms, cloſe, hot, f   ⸍ weather,
and much thunder and l ning. Thermometer high as in Augu... —Towards the
middle and latter part had generally moderate land and ſea breezes; and from the
18th had at leaſt one tornado every twenty-
four hours, which are always attended with
violent guſts of wind, thunder, lightning,
and exceſſive rain; but which greatly purify
                                              the

the air. Thermometer from 80° to 85°
and 90°.

October.—From the 1st to the 10th of
this month light variable winds all round
the compaſs, with frequent calms, thunder
and lightning, and very cloſe ſultry weather,
the clouds lowering very near the earth, and
the weight of the atmoſphere ſenſibly af-
fecting both the mind and body of the
Europeans and natives.—From the 10th to
the 21ſt had a heavy tornado every day,
with ſtrong land winds in the mornings
from the E. S. E. to E. N. E. which, towards ten o'clock, veered to the north and
north-weſt, and about noon to the weſt
and ſouth-weſt. The reſt of the month
had variable land and ſea breezes, with
frequent rain in the night, attended with
thunder and lightning, and in general very
hot, the thermometer ſeldom falling below
80° even in the night.

November.

November.—Early in this month the
fmokes began, which are noifome exhala-
tions attracted from the earth by the powerful heat of the fun, and have the appearance
of the fteam arifing from large breweries,
covering the whole face of Nature: the
weather at the fame time is extremely hot,
fultry, clofe, and oppreffive; and caufes fuch
an extreme laffitude, debility, and violent
perfpiration, that the whole body feels, as it
were, diffolving.—This is the moft fickly
feafon of the year; and even the natives
themfelves are not exempt from its baneful
influence. Fires and bark are the beft pre-
fervatives.—Strong land winds are frequent
during the fmokes.—Towards the latter end
of the month we had moderate and variable
land and fea breezes, with hazy weather,
frequent thunder and lightning, and an
appearance of fqualls or tornados from every
quarter of the compafs. We had only three

tornados

tornados this month, but one fo late as the 29th, which is rather uncommon.

December.—Till the 10th the weather continued as in the latter part of the preceding month; from the 10th to the 18th an almoft continued gale from the northeaft, and the fog or fmoke fo thick as to be totally impenetrable to the fun's meridian rays. During this period the air, raw, moift, and cold, is attended with the moft pernicious effects on the human body, totally checking the perfpiration, and caufing a dry and chapt hard fkin; and occafions alfo colds, fevers, and agues.—The birds and beafts feem to droop under its influence; no melody is heard in the woods, even the dove is filent: it has the fame effect on the earth as the froft in Europe, and caufes all kind of woods to fhrink in a moft aftonifhing manner. The thermometer feldom rifing above 75°.—Thefe winds are, by fome writers, called Haramatans, and are frequent

D along

along the African coaſt from December to March, but generally without the fog. The remainder of the month had little wind, chiefly from the north and north-weſt, with hazy and very hot weather; the thermometer in the ſhade at noon about 85°, expoſed to the ſun from 105° to 110.

The diſtinction of ſeaſons here is between the *rains* and *drys,* and I think the moſt natural diviſion of them compared with our own is as follows: *December, January, February, March, April, May,* the ſpring and ſummer, or dry ſeaſon: *June, July, Auguſt, September, October, November,* the winter and autumn, or rains and tornado ſeaſon. The tornados generally begin early in June, and continue till the middle or latter end of July: they commence again about the middle or beginning of October, and continue till the latter end of November. A remarkable circumſtance attending them is, that they always happen at or about

about the time of high or low water; from which it perhaps may appear they are influenced by the fame powers that caufe the flux and reflux of the fea.

From the foregoing account you will naturally conceive a very unfavourable idea of the climate; but the rains this year have been much more fevere and longer than they generally are; neither have the dry months been fo invariably fine as they commonly are.—I muft alfo obferve that my refidence, where I made my remarks, was at Sierra-Leone, and where the rains are always more fevere than they are any where along the coaft, occafioned by the high wood-crown'd mountains; and though we have, from the fame caufe frequent fhowers in the dry feafon, they are feldom felt from December to March, or April, a league from the coaft.

LETTER IV.

MY DEAR SIR,

I HOPE you have received my former letters, in which I endeavoured to give you
fuch a geographical and meteorological account of this country as my obfervations
furnifhed; I fhall now proceed to defcribe
the appearance of the country and its natural hiftory.

The fea coaft, except the peninfula of
Sierra-Leone, which is very high and mountainous, is generally a low fwamp covered
with very lofty ftraight mangroves, and interfected with innumerable little creeks.
As you approach the habitable and cultivated

vated part of the country, you find a boggy
plain covered with a thin fward, on which
grow a few ftraggling ftunted trees of the
ebony kind, without any fort of underwood. Thefe plains are overflowed by the
fea twice a year, at the vernal and autumnal
equinoxes, and depofit a mud from which
the natives extract falt by a fimple procefs.
When the cruft of mud left by the inunda-
tion is fufficiently hardened by the fun's
heat, they collect it together; it is then dif-
folved in water in large earthen pots: when
the water is fufficiently faturated with falt
it is boiled in fhallow brafs pans, and yields
an excellent falt, which, although not fo
white as that procured from fea water only,
by the fame method of boiling, is preferred
to it by the natives. Where their falt plains
are extenfive they employ their flaves, during the dry weather, in collecting the mud,
leaving a few old ones to boil it during the
rainy feafon.

D 3   The

The foil varies according to the fituation. In the level grounds it is a ftrong loam or ftiff clay; towards the uplands it is generally ftony, but every where exceedingly fertile. A faponaceous white earth is found in feveral parts of the country, which is of fo very unctious a nature that the natives frequently eat it with their rice, as it diffolves like butter; they alfo ufe it to white-wafh their houfes.

The face of the country, even where it is cultivated, appears woody from letting it lie fallow fix years out of feven; yet, in the interior parts, and in fome places near the fea, there are very extenfive Savannahs, where the grafs, known in the Weft Indies by the name of Guinea Grafs, grows to an amazing height; and feeds and conceals vaft numbers of deer, buffaloes, and elephants. The fame grafs is ufed by the natives to thatch their houfes ; and at the latter end of

the

the dry feafon is generally fet on fire, and when on fire burns with irrefiftible fury.

No country produces more variety of excellent and beautiful timber fit for every purpofe; but few, if any, bear the leaft affinity or refemblance to the woods of Europe.

The camwood tree is fo very plentiful in the interior country about the fources of the rivers, that I am informed the natives frequently burn it for fire-wood. And the tree which produces the gum copal grows in great abundance upon the heights of Sierra-Leone.

The palm tree, which furnifhes the natives with both wine and oil, flourifhes here in great plenty and perfection. The woods and mountains, as well as the favannahs, are well ftored with wild beafts and game. Lions are faid to be on the heights of Sierra-Leone; but I never yet faw any myfelf, nor have any perfons upon whofe veracity I could depend; but they have leopards

D 4   in

in abundance, equally fierce and rapacious as the lion. When preffed by hunger in the rainy feafon, they haunt the towns and villages in the night, particularly towards the dufk of the evening, and frequently carry off men as well as animals. If a leopard is fuccefsful in carrying off his prey undifturbed the firft night, he is fure to make an attempt the fucceeding one; they are then prepared for him, and he feldom efcapes. — They have likewife elephants, buffaloes, wild hogs amazingly fierce and large, deer of various kinds, fome very large and beautiful, others fmall like young antelopes (the flefh of all is very dry eating, and never fat): there are mufk cats, and a great variety of other animals, which the natives ufe for food; and monkies of fo many cafts and fpecies that it would require a volume to defcribe them; but there is one peculiarity attends them all, which is, when caught and kept only a few days in a houfe-

or

or ſhip, and then turned loofe, they never
return to the woods; for it is ſaid their old
companions would tear them to pieces. Indeed I have frequently feen the wild monkies chafe thofe that had been only a few
days caught, out of the ſkirts of the wood,
when they were fearching for food.

The Japanzees, or Chimpanzees, are alſo
natives of this country; and, when caught
young, become very tame and familiar; extremely fond of clinging to thofe they like,
and very fenſible of good, or ill treatment.
I have now a young one in my poffeffion;
who very readily comes when called by his
name; but if I puſh him, from me, or
ſtrike him, or even do not regard his advances by ſhewing him encouragement, he
turns ſullen and ſulky; will not take the
leaſt notice if called, or take any thing
from me, till I put him into good hu-
mour.—Their appearance, when they fit,
greatly reſembles that of an old negro, except

cept that the hair on their heads is ſtraight
and black like an Indian's; but their form
is ſo amply deſcribed in Brooke's Natural
Hiſtory, that I muſt refer you to it: however, a few other circumſtances related of
them may not be unentertaining—They
generally take up their abode near ſome de-
ſerted town, where the papau tree grows in
great abundance, of which they are very
fond; and build huts nearly in the form the
natives build their houſes, which they cover
with leaves; but this is only for the female
and young to lie in; the male always lies
on the outſide.—If one of them is ſhot the
reſt immediately purſue the deſtroyer of
their friend; and the only means to eſcape
their vengeance is to part with your gun,
which they directly ſeize upon with all the
rage imaginable, tear it to pieces, and give
over the purſuit.

Camelions, and great variety of lizards
and ſnakes, abound in this country: ſome

of

of the latter are extremely beautiful, but almoft all of them dangerous. I faw a boy upon the ifland of Banana's, who was bit by a fmall black fnake, about four or five feet long, as he was tending the goats and fheep, who died within two hours after receiving the wound. I examined it immediately after the boy was dead, but could difcern nothing more than two little punctures juft above the inftep, but not the leaft appearance of inflammation. I opened a vein in each arm, but no blood ran from the wounds, although the body remained as fupple as when living for feveral hours.

The moft remarkable fnakes are the *tenneé* for its fize, and the *finyacki-amoofong* for its pernicious quality.—The *tenneé*, when full grown, is from fifteen to twenty feet long, and about three feet round; the colour of the back dark grey; the belly fomething lighter and fpotted. It not only feizes upon and devours goats, fheep, and hogs, but the

the wild animals, such as leopards, tygers, and deer, are equally their prey where they come within their reach. The natives even affert that they are fo large in the favannahs, in the interior country, that they will fwallow a buffalo; though they are at no time formidable to man, except they fhould find him afleep.—The manner in which they take their prey is, by firft feizing the animal with their mouth, and as their teeth are turned inwards, like hooks, the more it ftruggles, the fafter it is held; they then throw their tails two or three times round the body of their victim, and, by a fudden contraction, break every bone. This, as the tail will not cover the whole carcafe, is performed by two or three operations: after which they make a circuit of at leaft half a mile round to fee that no enemy is near, particularly ants, who are the moft formidable to them; for, as they are perfectly inactive after having gorged their prey, if the

ants

ants find them in that situation, they soon
dispatch them by entering their mouth, ears,
and nose: but, if the coast is clear, they
then proceed to dress their prey, (if I may
be allowed the expression,) by besmearing
the whole carcase with an unctious kind of
saliva; and at the same time by licking it
into an oblong shape : after which they take
the head into their mouth, and suck the
whole gradually into their stomach without
the least mastication. When this is finished
the animal becomes as lifeless as a log, and
remains so till the whole is digested; which,
if the prey be large, takes three or four
days; during which time it is easily killed.—
I have known an instance of one being
killed a few hours after he had swal-
lowed a large goat with kid, which was
taken out whole and entire, except the
bones being broken, which appeared as
if they had gone through a mill. — They
generally frequent the savannahs and skirts

of

of towns; and are frequently seen rearing their heads above the grafs, which grows ten feet high, looking round for prey.—The natives efteem their flefh a great delicacy.

The *finyacki-amoofong* is a very fmall fnake, feldom exceeding a foot long, and about the thicknefs of a man's little finger; of a pale green colour, and black fpots.— This deftructive little creature is poffeffed of the power of ejecting a very fubtile vapour into the eyes of any animal that approaches it within the diftance of two or three feet, which inftantly occafions incurable blindnefs, and, for eight or ten days, caufes extreme pain. I have feen feveral people who have fuffered from them. But the moft formidable and deftructive enemy of man and beaft is the ant. Thefe creatures burft forth from their nefts in innumerable myriads: nothing can withftand their ravages, or turn them from their paths, but very large fires or deep water.

Frequent

Frequent inftances are known of their extinguifhing fire made to ftop their progrefs, by their numbers, and forming bridges, made by the facrifice of themfelves, to crofs fhallow waters which have impeded their route. They frequently oblige the natives to defert their habitations, and deftroy every thing upon the face of the earth, and under the earth, to a confiderable depth. In fhort, nothing efcapes or can withftand their alldevouring rage but metals.

The different fpecies of them are innumerable, from an inch in length to be fcarcely difcernible by the naked eye.

Many kinds burrow in the ground; fome erect their habitations of clay, in a conical form, upon the furface; and others build upon the branches and trunks of trees.

The *termite*, or white ant, called by the natives *bugabug*, is amply and accurately defcribed by Mr. Smeathman.

There

There is only one kind that I ever obferved to fly, and that only for a fhort time—they are a red ant, and generally fwarm towards evening and before rain. They do not fly far, and fhed their wings as foon as they alight.

Wild geefe and ducks, of various kinds, Guinea hens, pheafants, quails, curlues, plovers, fnipes, parrots, and great variety of doves and pigeons, are found in the woods and on the banks of rivers; befides an infinite affemblage of other birds, chiefly of beautiful plumage, and whofe notes vie with the feathered fongfters of Europe.

Their domeftic animals are cattle, fheep, goats, and fmall poultry.—Turkies, geefe, and Mufcovy and common ducks, would thrive here extremely well, and foon ftock the country, would the natives be at the trouble to rear them. And it is not a little furprifing that the Guinea fowls, which are real natives of the country, and are foon domefticated, fhould be neglected by them;

for

for it is never feen tame but in poffeffion of the Whites, or of thofe who adopt their manners.

The feas, rivers, and creeks, abound in great variety of moft excellent fifh. The *manatié*, or fea cow, is frequently taken in the rivers; they have alfo three kinds of frefh - water, and three of fea - turtle; befides feveral kinds of land tortoifes, and great abundance of excellent oyfters, which grow upon rocks, mud banks, and on the roots of mangroves; and are denominated mud, rock, or mangrove oyfters, from the place in which they are taken. They all are formed in bunches, and not fingle as ours.

Prawns, fhrimps, and crayfifh, are in great plenty and perfection; and feveral others, which ferve the natives for food, but are unknown in England.

Great numbers of alligators are bred in the creeks and rivers, which frequently carry off fmall cattle, and fometimes the perfons

E of

of the natives; yet fuch is their fuperftition, that, when a circumftance of that kind happens, they attribute it to witchcraft; and are fo infatuated, that they will not be at the pains to inclofe thofe parts of the rivers where their women and children are continually wafhing, and from whence they are frequently taken.—There are alfo vaft numbers of large fharks in the mouths of the rivers, which almoft inftantly feize upon any thing that falls overboard. This circumftance renders bathing, even in fhoal water, extremely dangerous. Yet even fharks and alligators, voracious as they are fuppofed to be, are harmlefs where they have not been ufed to prey upon animals.

In the river Gallienas, where alligators abound as much as they are faid to do in the Nile, they were never known to touch any body; though the natives were frequently fwimming in the river, till a flave fhip blew up off the mouth of the river a few

years

years ago. And at the Turtle iſlands, in the bay of Sherbro', an inſtance was never known of a ſhark attacking any perſon, although their children are playing in the water all day long. This the natives account for by being particularly careful to bury their dead, and their offals, at ſuch a diſtance from the ſea-ſide that the ſharks cannot even ſmell them.

The gall of the alligator is reckoned the moſt deadly poiſon, and in this the natives dip their poiſoned arrows. When an alligator is killed, the perſon who deſtroys it is obliged to have two witneſſes to prove he emptied the gall in their preſence.

No gold is found in this country: the little the women wear, as ornaments, is brought from a very great diſtance in the interior parts of the country, and is found in lumps waſhed down by the rains from the mountains. Neither have they any precious ſtones that I have yet heard of; but

that

that perhaps may be owing to their igno-
rance of them in their native ftate.

The loadftone is found in the high lands
of Sierra-Leone; and, from the appearance
of fome of the mountains, it is highly probable they may contain mines.

In the interior country, fouth of Sierra-
Leone, they have a white iron, very mal-
liable, of which they make knives and
fabres; and efteem it preferable to European
iron for every thing but edge tools. How
they fmelt and refine it from the ore, I
never could learn.

The beft indigo in the world, if we
may judge from the deep indelible blues
the natives give their cloths, grows wild
in every part of the country: and the Portuguefe, when fettled here, had large indigo works in feveral places, the ruins of
which are ftill remaining. They have alfo
the art of dying fcarlet and black in the
moft effectual manner.

Cotton

Cotton is cultivated by the natives, but in no greater quantity than they can manufacture themfelves; but, as it is an article that requires little trouble in the cultivation, I have endeavoured, by encouragement, to induce them to propagate it to fuch an extent as to become an article of European traffic. There are feveral kinds of it which materially differ, not only in quality but colour: particularly three kinds—one perfectly white, one of a tawny or Nankeen colour, and one of a pale red, or pink colour.

Sugar canes are a native plant, and grow wild to a fize beyond any I ever faw in the Weft Indies; they alfo have fome tobacco, which is not efteemed, owing perhaps to their want of knowledge in the cultivation. Rice is the chief and ftaple produce of the country, and conftitutes their principal and almoft only food: indeed fuch is their fondnefs for it, that the black failors, who, from their fituation, are fometimes

E 3 conftrained

conftrained to fubfift a few days upon falt beef and bifcuit, never fail to complain that they have been fo many days without food. Their method of cultivation, though at-tended with confiderable trouble, as they never cultivate the fame ground more than once in feven years, is performed in a very aukward and flovenly manner. After felecting a piece fit for their purpofe, they cut down the trees and bufhes, which when dry they fet fire to and burn, the afhes ferving for manure. The large old trees are always left ftanding, fo alfo are the ftumps of the fallen ones; and the trunks and large branches, unconfumed by the fire, are fuffered to remain as they fell. This is all the preparation they give the ground. — The firft new moon after the rains are well fet in, which here is the latter end of July, or beginning of Auguft, they fow their rice; after it is fown they flightly hoe it, juft fufficiently to cover the

grain;

grain: when it is about ten or twelve inches high they weed it, and in about eight weeks it is fit to reap. This is performed by cutting off the ears with a knife, and making it into ſmall ſheaves which they ſtick upon the branches of the fallen trees, till the weather is perfectly dry; they then ſtack it exactly as we do our corn. When wanted for uſe they ſtrip off the grain by hand, and boil it a little in water; it is afterwards well dried, and the huſk beat off in a large wooden mortar; and, where pains are taken with it, it is equally as white as Carolina rice, and every way preferable as an article of food. The whole management of the proceſs, after the rice is cut, is performed by the women. The ſides of hills are generally preferred for their rice plantations: and I have obſerved that the rice which grows on elevated or floping ſituations, though ſmaller grain, is much ſweeter, and more nutritive, than the pro-

E 4   duce

duce of low, moift, or level grounds, where the water lies longer on it; for, in Carolina and the Eaft Indies, they overflow their rice grounds. This method indeed is not un-known in this country; for, to the north-ward, about the Riopongeos, they have three rice harvefts in the year; one crop from the hills, and two from the plains which they overflow.

To fave labour, which the natives ftudi-oufly avoid as much as poffible, they plant their caffada, or manioc, amongft the rice after they have weeded it: it remains about four months in the ground, and is then fit for ufe. The young roots are very good eating either roafted or boiled, and are next to yams as a fubftitute for potatoes. The Abbe Raynal, in his hiftory of the Euro-pean fettlements in the Weft Indies, fays the manioc is twenty months in the ground before it attains perfection; and that it is a ftrong poifon before it has undergone the preparation

preparation neceſſary to make it into bread:
but this is by no means the caſe with the
African manioc, as it is eaten raw with as
much ſafety as roaſted or boiled. Indeed the
children are very fond of it raw, as it is very
ſweet when young.. Whether the Abbe
gives us his account of the Weſt Indian
manoic from hear-ſay or experience I know
not; but what he advances as the cauſe of
the black colour of the natives of Africa is
utterly without foundation.

Rice, as I before obſerved, is the principal food of the natives, although they have
caſſada, yams, eddies, ſweet potatoes, and
great variety of other roots and vegetables
unknown in Europe; particularly two kinds,
which grow upon large trees; one very much
reſembles a ſweet potatoe in form and taſte,
the other eats ſomething like a bean, and
has nearly the ſame ſhape, except only one
of the kind grows in a pod, which is much
larger than the common bean, and rounder.

The

The Mollugo, or African chick-weed, which produces a fmall bean, grows in fuch quantities, that, during the rains, or after a flood in the country, the fhores are covered with them; and vaſt bodies, of feveral acres in extent, are feen floating many leagues out at fea; and thefe alfo ferve the natives for food in times of fcarcity.—Indian corn and millet both thrive extremely well, but are little cultivated.

The Malagato pepper, or grain of Paradife, is found in the woods; but it is not fo pungent as that which is purchafed from the natives at Baffa and the places adjacent. The bird and pod pepper is cultivated in great plenty and perfection; and there are feveral kinds of aromatic fruits, which are excellent fubftitutes in culinary ufes for the fpices of the Eaft.

Moſt of the tropical fruits known in the Weſt Indies abound here in the greateſt perfection; particularly pine-apples, oranges,

oranges, and limes; which are in feafon,
but not in the fame degree of plenty, all
the year round. Guavas, tamarinds, aca-
jous, or, as the Englifh call them, cafhews,
and cocoa-nuts, have been planted by Europeans, and thrive amazingly. The wild
fig-tree grows to the fize of an oak; but the
fruit is fmall, and generally deftroyed by the
ants. Nothing can exceed the luxuriancy
of the wild vines, which bear amazing
quantities of grapes, beautiful to the eye,
but of an acrid tafte. If cultivated, however, they would, no doubt, be equal to
thofe of Europe. Several kinds of plums·
and other fruits, cooling and grateful, are
found in the woods, which are unknown
either in Europe or the Weft Indies.

But the principal fruit, in the eftimation of
the natives, is the cola'. Both the tree and
fruit in external appearance very much
refemble the walnut. The fruit grows in
large clufters, which contain fix or eight
colás.

colás. On the outfide it is covered with a
thick tough rind, and a thinner white rind
on the infide : when this is taken off it divides into two parts, and is either of a
purple colour or white; but the former is
generally preferred. Its tafte refembles the
Peruvian bark, and its virtues are faid to be
the fame. Thofe who can procure it chew
it at all times and at all feafons. It is prefented to guefts at their arrival and departure — fent in complimentary prefents to
chiefs — is a confiderable article of inland
trade, as well as with the Portuguefe from
Baffou', and frequently made the token of
peace or war. — It grows in the greateft
plenty and perfection in the river Scarcies
and on the Bullam fhore, oppofite to Sierra-
Leone.

Caftor nuts and many others, which produce oil, grow fpontaneoufly almoft every
where; and the leaves of the caftor are a
moft

moſt excellent application in ſwellings and
bruiſes.

Water is the only beverage the natives
drink at their meals; nor have they yet
found the means of intoxicating themſelves
with any thing of their own produce, but
palm wine.

The natives, however, of the Riopongeos
are to be excepted; who make a ſtrong
heady beer from a root called ningeé. It is
extremely bitter, not much unlike the beer
made in Ruſſia and Norway. The plant is
cultivated, and ſeems to partake of the
nature of the aſbeſtos, in not being altered or
conſumed by the action of fire.—The root,
which is the only part uſeful, grows to the
ſize of a man's leg, and three or four feet
long. The preparation of it for brewing is
as follows—They dig a ſquare hole in the
ground; and firſt place a layer of dry man-
grove-wood cleared of its bark, then a layer
of the root, which has been previouſly well
waſhed

wafhed and dried; and fo proceed till the
place is full, which they cover over very
clofe with fods, leaving only a fmall aper-
ture at the bottom for the air and fire.
When it is fufficiently burnt, which is
known by the wood's being entirely con-
fumed, they carefully remove the fods from
the top, to preferve the afhes which they
make ufe of, and the root is taken out, and
again well wafhed and dried. — When
wanted for ufe it is pounded with a heavy
wooden mallet, and fteeped in water till
its virtues are extracted. The water is
then boiled, and afterwards put into earthen
pots to ferment. When the fermentation
is over it is fit to drink.—The whole procefs takes up about three days. The root,
when raw, is fo extremely acrid as to exco-
riate the mouth on the flighteft touch;
except it be eaten with the afhes of a former
burning, which is a ftrong alkali.

The

The beer is a powerful diuretic, and confidered by the natives as a fpecific in the venereal diforder.

In fhort, my friend, Nature appears to have been extremely liberal, and to have poured forth her treafures with an unfparing hand : but in moft cafes the indolence of the natives prevents their reaping thofe advantages, of which an induftrious nation would poffefs themfelves.

I fhall conclude with wifhing you every happinefs;

And am,

DEAR SIR,

Yours, &c.

LETTER

LETTER V.

MY DEAR FRIEND,

IN my laſt letter, which I hope you received ſafe, I endeavoured to give you an
account of ſuch parts of the natural hiſtory
of this country as my obſervation furniſhed.
In this I ſhall proceed to relate ſueh particulars as I have been able to collect, of
their religion, laws, government, and wars.

It is hardly poſſible for an European to
form an adequate idea of the religion of the
Pagan inhabitants of this country; for they
have no order of prieſts, nor any fixed object of adoration which might be termed a
national worſhip; every man faſhions his
own divinities according to his fancy: and

the

the imagination can scarcely conceive the monstrous, uncouth, and ridiculous figures they adore.

They acknowledge and profess their belief in a God, who, they say dwells above them, and made and governs all things. If any circumstance of joy or distress happen they very cooly say God sent it them (unless they fancy it was caused by witchcraft); but without having any idea of returning God thanks for a benefit, or, by submission and prayer, of endeavouring to deprecate his wrath. They make offerings indeed to their devils and genii, who they suppose are the executive ministers of the Deity. Their devils, who they imagine reign paramount upon earth, are small images of clay, often renewed and made in some resemblance of a man: these are placed at the foot of a tree, and a small shed of dry leaves is constructed over them: various offerings are made to them of bits of cloth, pieces of broken

F   cups,

cups, plates, mugs, or glaſs bottles, braſs
rings, beads, and ſuch articles, but I never
obſerved any thing of value given to them;
indeed when they want to render their
devil propitious to any undertaking, they
generally provide liquor; a very ſmall liba-
tion is made to him, and the reſt they drink
before his altar.

Beſides theſe devils they have images of
wood from eight to twelve inches long,
painted black, which are their *lares* (houſe-
hold gods); but they ſeem to pay very little
attention to any of them, except when
they think they ſtand in need of their aſſiſt-
ance.

On every accident which befalls them,
whether trivial or important, they make an
offering to their genii, who they imagine
inhabit, and have power, in the air, as the
devils have upon earth. A braſs pan faſtened to the ſtump of a tree by driving a
country axe through it—a glaſs bottle ſet
up

up on the stump of a tree—a broken bottle placed upon the ground with two or three beads in it, covered with a bit of cloth, and surrounded with stones—a rag laid upon small sticks and covered with a broken calabash—and a long slip of cloth, generally white, tied to the end of a pole and stuck upright in the ground, are the offerings they generally make; and in the efficacy of which, for whatever purpose they are made, they have implicit faith. To remove one of them, even unknowingly, is a great offence, and subjects the aggressor to a *pala-ver*, or action in their courts of law; who, if he be a poor man, and the offended person be powerful, the crime is often only to be expiated by the loss of liberty. Such are a part; for it would be impossible to describe the whole, of the ceremonies of a religion, if it may be so termed, in which it is difficult to determine which is most predominant, folly or superstition.

F 2 The

The Mandingoes who profefs the Mahometan religion, are, in outward appearance,
ftrict followers of the precepts of the Alcoran; nor could Mahomet himfelf have
wifhed for more zealous promoters of his
law. Fully fenfible of what importance it
is to have the confcience in keeping, they
neglect no means of policy to fpread their
religious doctrines—where they are ftrong
they ufe coercive meafures; and where they
are not in a capacity to exert thofe means, they
ufe every art that human fubtilty can fuggeft.—In the villages of the tribes around
them they erect fchools, and teach their
youth gratis, to read and write Arabic;
and their miffionaries, by temporizing with
the prevailing follies and foibles of the diftant nations which they vifit; by affuming
to themfelves the fanctity and authority of
the fervants of God; by abftaining from all
ftrong liquors; and, above all, by pretend-
ing to have power over every fpecies of
witchcraft;

witchcraft; and, by their trade in making charms, do fo infinuate themfelves into the confidence of the chiefs and principal people; that I never vifited a town in this part of Africa where I did not find a Mandingo man as prime minifter, by the name of *book.nan*, without whofe advice nothing was tranfacted.

The religion of Mahomet was propagated in this country by the Arabs and Foolahs. Many of the Arab priefts, or faquins travel not only acrofs the country from the banks of the Nile, but alfo from Morocco to Abiffinia, and are fupported by the charity of the nations through which they pafs. During my former refidence in the interior part of the Mandingo country, I faw feveral of them, and gained no little efteem from the natives, by the alms I beftowed upon thofe travelling mendicants, who never eat or fleep in a houfe during their peregrina-

F 3   tion.

tion. By means of thefe people, and the
travelling black merchants, the defeat of the
Spaniards before Gibraltar was known at
the Riopongeos within forty days after the
action.

Circumcifion of male children, whether
a religious or political inftitution, is in general, but not univerfally practifed all over
Africa: but the circumcifion of females I
never yet read or heard of in any country,
but among the Suzeés and Mandingoes:
with them both fexes undergo the operation
when they arrive at the age of puberty; and
the performance of this fingular rite on the
females is by cutting off the exterior point
of the *clitoris*. The ceremonies attending
it are very curious :—Every year during the
dry feafon, and on the firft appearance of a
new moon, the girls of each town who are
judged marriageable are collected together;
and, in the night preceding the day on
which the ceremony takes place, are conducted

ducted by the women of the village into
the inmoft receffes of a wood. Griggories, or charms, are placed at every
avenue or path which might lead to the
confecrated fpot, to warn and deter the approach of the ignorant or defigning, during
their confinement, which continues one
moon and one day. They are feen by no
perfon but the old woman who performed
the operation, and who brings them their
provifions daily; fhould fhe, through fick-
nefs, or any other caufe, be unable to attend, the perfon who is fubftituted in her
place calls out with a loud voice as fhe approaches, leaves the victuals at a certain
fpot, and retires unfeeing or unfeen; for,
fhould any perfon, either through accident
or defign, break into their retirements, death
is the punifhment annexed.

It is principally during their confinement
in the wood, when the body is fubdued by
pain, and the mind foftened by the gloomy

ftillnefs

ftillnefs of every thing around them, that they are taugh the religious cuftoms and fuperftitions of their country; for, till that period, they are not thought capable of underftanding or practifing them.—When the time deftined for their continuance in the wood is expired, which is judged fufficient for the healing their wounds, they are brought into the town in the night, where they are received by all the women of the village, young and old, quite naked: in this ftate, and in a kind of irregular proceffion, with various inftruments of national mufic, they parade the ftreets till break of day; and fhould any man be found even peeping during their peregrination, he would immediately fuffer death, or pay a flave.—A probation of one moon fucceeds their releafe from the wood; during which they are every day conducted in proceffion, with mufic, and their heads and bodies covered, to every principal perfon's houfe in the town,

before

before which they dance and fing till they
are prefented with fome trifling prefent.
At the expiration of the month they are
releafed from further attendance, and immediately given to the men deftined for
their hufbands.

How they came to adopt, or for what
reafon they practife, this very fingular rite, I
never could learn; but the women hold it
in fuch veneration, that to be reproached
with the want of it, is the moft villifying
term they can poffibly ufe; and frequent
inftances occur of women in years fub-
mitting to the operation, who, though born
in other countries, yet, coming to refide
where it was practifed, were expofed to the
reproach.

Their government and their laws appear to have been originally of the patri-
archal kind, where the elder of every family
was prieft and judge. Time, that changes
all

all things, has made fome change in this alfo.

At prefent the prevailing form in thefe parts of Africa is a kind of mixed monarchy, eleƈtive, and extremely limited both in external and internal power; and very much refembles the authority of the mayor of a corporation town in England; for the word *mungo,* which the Europeans tranflate *king,* only fignifies head man; and he is always addrefled by the title of *fafeé,* or *father.* Every feparate diftriƈt, in the fame nation, has a feparate king, ruler, or chief.

The Suzee's and Mandingoes, indeed, who are the moft powerful and numerous, acknowledge fubjeƈtion to the king of the Foolahs, whom they reprefent as a powerful prince, whofe empire is very extenfive, reaching from Gambia to Cape Mount; but the Bullams, Timaneys, and Bagoes, acknowledge no power fuperior to their own.

.The

The neceſſary qualifications for any perſon to aſcend the throne are, a thorough
knowledge of the local cuſtoms of the
country; to be a good orator; to have a
clear underſtanding, or, as they emphati-
cally expreſs it, to have a good head; to
be ſober, to be at all times ready and
attentive to hear the complaints and re-
dreſs the grievances of the ſubjeƈt; and to
be ſufficiently powerful in his own ſlaves
and people, who live under his immediate
proteƈtion, to enforce the obſervance and
execution of the laws.

Except among the Mandingoes and
Suzeés, few kings are natives of the countries they govern. So different are their
ideas from ours, that very few are ſolicitous
of the honour, and competition is very
ſeldom heard of.

The reigning prince has the power of
appointing a deputy, who, upon his death,
ſucceeds to all his honours and authority;
and

and governs, in his name, till they elect a
new king.—If the deputy be a man of
power and addrefs, he often takes poffeffion
of the property alfo of the deceafed king,
and fecures it till the new king is elected,
who will adjudge it to the right heir. But
it frequently happens that if the deputy is
found equal to the tafk of governing, he is
either confirmed in the dignity of king, or
continues to act under the title of deputy as
long as he lives.

The prefent ruler of Sierra-Leone, who is
in fact only a deputy, has reigned in that capacity for more than ten years; and his
fubjects are fo well pleafed with his conduct
that they wifh to make him king : but he
appears to be perfectly fatisfied in ruling
with a fubordinate title.—The revenue, or
rather the emoluments of his office, arife
from the prefents made him on every occafion where his affiftance or authority are
wanted; and which are always propor-
tioned

tioned to the ability of the giver and the importance of the affair.—From a poor man, for inftance, a bafket of rice, a couple or half a dozen fowls, or a goat, would be accepted; but nothing lefs than the value of a flave would be taken in an affair of confequence.

The enfigns of authority of the kings of Sherbro' are an elephant's tail carried before them; or, if it be fent by a meffen-ger, it has the fame obedience paid to it as to the fign manual. But I never obferved any fuch tokens of royalty among the other kings, except what they received from the whites; fuch as a filver-headed cane, or a gold-laced hat.

Though the executive power and final decifion of all caufes is vefted in the king, yet every head, or principal man of a village, thinks himfelf fole lord within his own town. Neither can the king com-mand, but only intreat, except in matters

which

which have been debated and determined upon in full council. For inftance, I wanted fome wood at a diftance from my refidence, and fent people to cut it, the head man of the diftrict prevented them; I complained to the king; his anfwer (which I found to be true) was, he would fend to the man to defire him to let my people cut the wood; but that the place belonged to him, and he had no authority to compel him.

The family of a deceafed king, or head man, lay no claim to fuperiority over their countrymen from their office, but fill that ftation only in which their wealth or connexions place them; and it very often happens that the fon of a deceafed chief, a few days after his father's death, is neceffitated to hire himfelf as a gremeta, or failor, to an European trader, for fubfiftance.

Prefent poffeffion is the only tenure they allow of in the occupying of lands. If a

man

man quits his fituation, another may immediately take poffeffion, provided he is a native ; for they are extremely tenacious of their rights, and will not fuffer any ftrangers to fettle among them without their confent and approbation.

Their laws, handed down by tradition from father to fon, are merely the local cuftoms of the country; which differ, but not very effentially, in every diftrict or ftate.—All caufes are tried by the king, affifted by the head men, in open *burret*, or court ; and there are a fet of men called *palaver talkers*, (i. e. *counfellors*) who plead on both fides.—I have known one of thefe men fpeak for two hours with fuch dignity of action, force and energy of elocution, as would do honour to an Englifh orator.

Difputes among themfelves, when brought to a *palaver*, are generally decided with equity, according to the evidence produced;

particularly

particularly if the parties are equal in power; and the lofing party pays all damages and cofts of fuit before he goes out of court, or is obliged to give good fecurity.

In their difputes with white men they are not very rigid obfervers of juftice ; and, what is fomething fingular, if a white man fhould fucceed in his fuit, he reaps no other advantage from it than the honour of being in the right; as they never adjudge any re-compenfe to be made him on any occafion ; and, right or wrong, he muft pay the expences.—I have often afked them the reafon of this conduct; they only anfwered, " White men get too much money; they " cannot want their money."

All capital offences are punifhed with either fine flavery, or death; but the latter is now feldom practifed, except among the Man-dingoes, who rule by the Mahometan law, and whofe proceedings are always fum-mary; or, in cafes of murder, when the

friends

friends of the deceafed take vengeance before the crime has been publicly judged.

Witchcraft is flavery inevitable; but poifon, adultery, or any other crime, may be
compenfated by fine.

The method of recovering debts appears
to be founded upon the firft principles of
jurifprudence, which are generally adopted
by all nations.

Debts are commonly contracted for a limited time; that is, there is fuch a length
of credit given. If the debtor refufes or
delays payment when the debt is due and
demanded, the creditor applies to the king,
or chief, for his affiftance; who fends to
the debtor, defiring him to pay the debt.
If after this notice from the king, he refufes to pay it, or to fatisfy his creditor,
the latter gets the king's confent to feize
the perfon of his debtor, or any of his flaves
or people. If this be found impracticable,
by the debtor's living in another town, the

G   creditor

creditor feizes upon any perfon, who refides in the fame town as the debtor, and detains that perfon till the debt is paid, which the people of the town compel the debtor to do immediately.

And this is not all; for when a man is thus deprived of his liberty for the debt of another, he inftantly brings a palaver, or action, againft the real debtor, and generally recovers confiderable damages, as a compenfation for the imprifonment.

The moft fingular law I have yet obferved in Africa is what they term the purrah, and is peculiar to Sherbro'. This wife, political inftitution is diffeminated through the country for the purpofe of putting an end to difputes and wars, as the jealoufy, pride, and irritability of the natives are fuch as will not fuffer them, even when confcious of being the aggreffors, to make conceffions. Any freeman, after a certain age, (fuppofed about thirty) may become a member of this affociation. On his

his admiffion into the fociety he undergoes various ceremonies, and is enjoined the ftricteft fecrefy refpecting them, which they preferve as inviolably as the free mafons in Europe do the myfteries of their inftitution; and to which it has fome refemblance in other refpects; particularly in having a grand mafter, or head purrah man, in every diftrict or ftate, and the non-admiffion of females. This law is never ufed but in the dernier refort; and when it is in force, the crimes of witchcraft and murder are punifhable by it.

When two tribes, or nations, are at war, and begin to be tired, or wifh to put an end to it, but are too haughty and proud to make overtures to each other, they apply to the ruler of a neighbouring ftate for his interference as a mediator: if the offer be accepted, he immediately fends to the contending parties, to inform them he will act as umpire if they chufe to refer their dif-

putes to him; and that if they do not
agree to terminate their differences amica-
bly, he will fend for the purrah, as he will
no longer look on with indifference, and
fee thofe who ought to be friends deftroy
each other and depopulate their country,

Should they, after this meffage, prove re-
fractory, the purrah is ordered out; and the
grand fundamental article of the purrah law
is, that no blood fhall be fhed while it is in
force; fo that the late contending parties
follow their feveral occupations without fear.
But rencounters fometime happen, as their
vindictive and revengeful difpofition will
feldom fuffer them to let flip an opportunity
of gratifying their thirft of vengeance, even
under the terror of this law.

When the aggreffors are known to the
purrah, they come down in a body of forty
or fifty men armed and difguifed. All perfons, of every age or defcription, fly before
them; and if they find any perfon out of
their

their houfes, they put them to death, or
difpofe of them in fuch a manner that they
are never more heard of. This is alfo the
fate of all tranfgreffors of the purrah law,
when feized by the people of this extraordinary affociation.

It is impoffible to defcribe the dread and
terror this inftitution ftrikes into the common people: they believe the purrah men
are poffeffed of the power of the devils, and
can do whatever mifchief they pleafe without being affected by it themfelves. They
take away the ftock and provifions, or
whatever they like, belonging to the natives, without the leaft interruption or fubfequent inquiry.

In defcribing the cuftoms and manners
of diftant nations, we are under a neceffity
of ufing fuch expreffions and phrafes as fuit
our own idioms. Hence every petty quarrel,
when perhaps there is only ten or a dozen
combatants on each fide, is in Africa called

a war.

a war. It is the fame alfo in fpeaking of
their chiefs, or head men, who are all dig-
nified by the Europeans with the title
of king.

The vindictive and violent fpirit of revenge which every African poffeffes when
he imagines he is injured or infulted, is the
caufe of frequent wars among the natives.
When a national war is agreed upon, it becomes general, and every perfon of each
party is equally obnoxious to the other; but
their petty wars, or quarrels, only involve
the particular town, or towns, which are
engaged.—Their expeditions are always of
the predatory kind. To furprize and burn
a village, and make a few prifoners, is the
utmoft extent of their ambition; they never
attempt to meet each other in the field, but
fculk about in ambufh, and laugh at the
folly of the Europeans, when told of the
manner in which they fight, and the numbers they bring into the field; as an African
army

army feldom exceeds 500 men, and even
that is confidered as a very large one. The
young men only go to war; but they are
very indifferent foldiers, and can only be
kept together with the hope of plunder, or
being well fupplied with liquor.

They are fometimes two or three years
preparing and forming alliances with the
neighbouring tribes before they make an
attack, which is commonly done juft at the
commencement of the rains, when the men
are employed in their plantations; at which
time they are fure of finding the towns de-
fencelefs.

When two tribes, or nations are negoti-
ating, and the final refult muft be peace or
war; and, when they have made their elec-
tion, if for war, two red *cold* are depofited
upon a ftone at the place of meeting; if for
peace, one white *cold* is left at the fame
place, which is divided into two parts, each
party take one piece, and they then meet

each

each other without fear to adjuſt the particulars.

The inhabitants of the ſea coaſt have almoſt totally laid aſide their national weapons for the ſabre and gun ; but the natives of the inland countries ſtill uſe the ſpear, dart, and poiſoned arrow.

It does not appear that the intercourſe which has ſo long ſubſiſted between the Africans and Europeans has made any material change in their cuſtoms or manners, except giving them a reliſh for ſociety, and the enjoyment of what they conſider as the luxuries of life, European manufactories, I have endeavoured to diſcover the cauſes of their wars, and whether the accuſation ſo often made, — that the natives of Africa were excited to make war upon each other by the Europeans who traded with them— was, or was not, founded in fact. And this, I am free to declare, never was the caſe in any inſtance which fell under my obſervation ;

tion: and from every account I could collect
it never had been the cafe.

When I firft arrived at the Ifles de Lofs,
I found an almoft general war raged
throughout the extent to which we traded.
The Suzeés, aided by the Mandingo flaves
who had revolted from their mafters, were
at war with the Bagoes and Mandingoes;
and the people of Sherbro' were at war
with each other. The origin of the war
between the Suzeés and Bagoes, and their
allies, arofe from a Bagoe man killing a
native of a Suzeé town, where he at that
time refided: he fled from their refentment
among his countrymen, who refufed to deliver him up to the friends of the perfon he
had killed, agreeable to the laws of the
country. The war in Sherbro' arofe from
a quarrel between two chiefs, and involved
the whole country in their difpute. After
fixing my eftablifhment at Sierra-Leone, I
made a trip into Sherbro', in a mediato al
capacity,

capacity, to endeavour to terminate their disputes. I visited both the principals in person, and sent to the allies of both parties. Reciprocal presents passed between us; but such was the mutual jealousy and distrust of each party, that I never could prevail on them to meet each other on board my vessel, though they separately visited me. I had however the satisfaction to lay the foundation of a truce, which has continued ever since, and is now enforced by the purrah.

LETTER

LETTER VI.

Sierra-Leone, Nov, 20, 1786.

DEAR SIR,

My laſt letter conveyed to you the beſt accounts I could give of the religion, laws, and government, of the inhabitants of this country; in this I ſhall endeavour to deſcribe the perſons of the natives, and ſuch of their particular cuſtoms and ceremonies which have fallen under my own obſervation, or which I have received from perſons upon whoſe veracity I can depend.

It is a general remark all along the coaſt of Africa, that thoſe nations bordering upon the ſea, or inhabiting iſlands, are a much ſtouter, better made, a braver, and more

active

active people than thofe who refide in the interior parts of the country. This, perhaps, may be in fome meafure accounted for by the difference of food, thofe upon the fea-coaft living a good deal upon fifh, and breathing a more falubrious air.

The Bullams, Timmaneys, and Bagoes, are a ftout, active, and perfonable race; of a good black, ftraight limbs, and pleafing features; and rather above the middle fize. The Timmaneys, in particular, are remarkable for an open, ingenuous countenance; and many of their women are really handfome.

During my refidence here I have only feen two deformed people, and their misfortunes were occafioned by accidents in their infancy.

The Suzees are of a yellow caft; and in perfon much inferior to thofe I have juft mentioned; though they are generally straight

ſtraight limbed, they have thick lips and
flatter noſes.

The Mandingoes ſeem to be a diſtinſt
race from any of the others : they, are
tall and ſlender, of an indifferent black,
and remarkably ſmall eyes : they wear
their beards like the Jews in Europe.

The Suzeés, Bullams, &c. ſhave while
they are young; but, when their hair begins
to turn grey, they ſuffer their beards to
grow; for the ſilver tokens of age with
them denote wiſdom : and, indeed, ſome
of their old men, with long white beards,
ſeated in council, make a moſt venerable
appearance.

The ſtriking difference between the free
people I have deſcribed, and the appearance
of the plantation ſlave, is ſo great, that I
was never miſtaken in my opinion reſpeſt-
ing their ſituation even at firſt ſight.

The free man, elated by his liberty,
walks with dignity and conſcious pride, and
looks

looks with an eye of confidence on all around — while the flave, on the contrary, oppreffed by the confideration of his fituation, moves on with humble ftep and down-caft eye.

The perfons of the flaves (except fuch as were born on the fea coaft) are generally lefs in ftature, and not fo robuft or well made as the native free men, and come from the interior part of the country.

The Foolahs, who inhabit the country on the back of the nations I have defcribed, appear to be an intermediate race between the Arab and the black, and very like the Eaft Indian Lafcar, having long, ftraight, black hair, yellow complexion, thin face, and long Roman nofes. They are ftrict followers of the Alcoran; and, by their wars for the propagation of their religion, furnifh a great number of the flaves which are fold in thefe parts.

Voltaire,

Voltaire, in his preliminary difcourfe, mentions a race of people inhabiting the interior parts of Africa, whom he calls Albinos, and reprefents them as being of a milky white colour, and diminutive ftature. I have made the moft diligent inquiry of the natives, and travelling black merchants, but never could gain the leaft information that fuch a people exifted. But I have feen feveral white negroes in different parts of Africa of a milky, or chalky whitenefs, and white wool; but thefe do not propagate their likenefs, but have black children, and are only confidered as *lufus naturæ*. I remember to have feen one of the fame kind in Georgia, South Carolina, and one in England, they were both females.

The Suzeé language feems to be the root from which the Bagoe, Bullam, and Timmaney is fprung; it is foft, and abounds with vowels and labial founds. The Mandingo language is, as the people are, perfectly

fectly different from any of the others, and appears to me to be a corrupt Arabic, though not the same as they teach in their schools, which they term the language of prayer.

The difposition of the natives is nearly fimilar every where, extremely indolent, unlefs excited by revenge, of implacable tempers, full of treachery and diffimulation, where they conceive the leaft refentment; nor do they ever let flip an opportunity of gratifying their thirft of vengeance when they can do it with impunity. To their particular friends indeed, they are hofpitable and kind; but are addicted to pilfering, and are remarkable for the ficklenefs of their conduct on almoft every occafion.

The Mandingoes, from religious motives, hate a Chriftian, and vilify thofe Europeans who refide among them, and whom they frequently fee drinking and rioting, with the appellation of dog. But when I formerly

formerly refided among them, by purfuing a contrary conduct, and by being enabled to converfe with them on the tenets of their religion, I received fuch treatment from them in the time of the utmoft dif- trefs, when I was dangeroufly ill, as I could have expected only from my beft and deareft friends.

Their methods of falutation are various; when a flave approaches his mafter to pay him obedience he bends the right knee almoft to the ground, and ftretches out his right arm, with the hand fhut, which he fupports with the left hand under the elbow. When two friends, or equals, meet, they put their right hand upon their breafts and wifh each other good day; and fome- times embrace, or fhake hands, and fnap the finger and thumb. When a ftranger comes upon a vifit to a friend, no notice is taken of him till he announces his vifit in form, which is often four or five days after

H   his

his arrival, during which time he is provided with every thing neceſſary for himſelf
and people, apart from the family: the
ſame cuſtom is obſerved, by their ambaſſa-
dors, or public meſſengers, upon buſineſs of
importance. When the women meet upon
viſits, they join their right hands and curtſy;
but the young and unmarried embrace
with the moſt ſeeming affection. When a
ſon viſits his mother after an abſence, and
the firſt ſalutation is over, he lies at her
feet, and, while ſhe carefully examines his
head for the purpoſe of deſtroying vermin,
he relates the adventures of his journey.

The women are exceedingly clean in
their perſons, and are ſtrictly attentive to
domeſtic duties; and none can be more
fond or careful of their offspring, or make
better nurſes. They never wean their children till they are able to walk, and to carry
a calabaſh of water to their mother, which
they inſtruct them to do as ſoon as poſſible;

for,

for, during the time a child is at the breaft,
the woman is not permitted to cohabit with
her hufband, as they fuppofe it would be
prejudicial to her milk. Barrennefs they
dread as the greateft reproach; and Nature
has exempted them from the pain and forrow
our fair countrywomen experience in child-
birth, as they are feldom confined more
than a few hours. In their domeftic amufe-
ments they, in fome refpect imitate the good
country houfewife in England. In the evening the head-wife, furrounded by the reft
of her hufband's women, and her female
attendants, is employed in fpinning and
carding cotton, while one of the company
amufes the reft with telling ftories upon
the plan of Æfop's fables: to thefe tales I
have often liftened with infinite pleafure.
They have feveral games of chance, at
which the men and women play feparate;
but both fexes are paffionately fond of
dancing, which they never fail to enjoy

when

when they have a light moon and fair
weather, from an hour after fun-fet, till
midnight. Befides this, the birth of a child,
or the arrival of a friend or relation, furnifhes them with an opportunity of enjoy-
ing their favourite amufement of finging
and dancing, which they term a *cullunjee*.
When a *cullunjee* is performed on any great
occafion, they introduce dancers drefied in a
grotefque ftyle; on their heads they wear a
high cap made of rufhes, ftuck round
with feathers, and their faces are painted
about the eyes, nofe, and mouth, with
chalk, or white clay, and they wear a petty-
coat of rufhes round their waift, which in
dancing fpreads in every direction. In
their hands they have pieces of flat wood,
which they clap together, and with which
they keep time during the dance.

The death of a child, friend, or relation,
adds no lefs to the enjoyment of this paftime,
by performing the wha', or cry : but, from

the

the manner in which it is performed, a ftranger to their ceremonies would rather term it a rejoicing.

On the evening of the day appointed the friends and relations of the deceafed affemble together, and proceed, by a flow and folemn movement, to an open fpace before their houfes. Here they begin finging the praifes of the deceafed, and dancing to the mufic of a drum. In the dance they frequently vary the figure; fometimes forming one great circle round the mufic, and clapping hands at every period or repetition of their fong. Sometimes one perfon performs the dance, the reft fitting or ftanding round in a circle, joining chorus and clapping hands as before: at other times two, three, or four, will dance together till they are weary, and then are relieved by others; the reft finging and clapping hands. This, with firing of guns, continues from evening till near daylight, without intermiffion; but

H 3 they

they frequently regale themselves with liquor and tobacco. This ceremony is repeated three nights succeſſively.

For people of conſequence, whoſe friends can afford it, the cry is repeated once or twice a year for ſeveral years; but the poorer ſort are ſometimes two or three years before they can procure means to purchaſe rum and tobacco ſufficient for the purpoſe : but whatever time they may be before they are enabled to put it in excu-tion, it is never omitted.

This may be termed the public mourn-ing after the death of their friends or rela-tions, in which both ſexes join; but there is alſo another kind, of a more private nature, practiſed by the women only, and is pecu-liar to the Bullams and Timmaneys only.

The mourners wear a white linen or cotton cap, which is drawn over their eyes in ſuch a manner as to prevent their ſeeing any thing, except on the ground, without turning their heads quite up, and ſeveral

ſtrings

ftrings of large country beads are faftened round their neck and waift.—If married women, they are ftripped of their cloth, and allowed to wear the *tuntungee* only.

They are not fuffered to eat or drink with any other perfon, or cook their own victuals, but at meal times beat a drum and dance before the perfon's door who is to give it them; and nobody is allowed even to eat or drink out of the veffels they make ufe of.

The time this kind of mourning con-tinues is not fixed, but regulated by the whim and caprice of the perfon who orders it, who is generally the mother, aunt, or fome elderly relation; and is commonly performed by girls approaching the age of marriage, in order to preferve their chaftity; for fhould any intercourfe between the fexes be difcovered, during the continuance of this ceremony, the woman would be-

come

come infamous, and the man be liable to a severe punifhment.

A woman alfo, when fhe fuppofes her hufband neglects her, has the privilege of putting his favourite miftrefs into mourning. When this, however, happens, after a fhort probation and a peace-offering, to the wife, of a goat or fix fowls, a jar of liquor, and a little tobacco, to be ufed in a cullunjeé, fhe is reftored to his arms.

Indeed this appears no bad policy on the part of the elderly wives, to preferve fome degree of confequence with the men; for during the time the young woman is in this mourning, the hufband is deprived of her fociety.

They have various kinds of national mufic; but the drum feems to be the principal inftrument, of which they have three forts, but they are of different fizes, according to the ufe for which they are intended: one is made of a hard wood, which is hol-

lowed,

lowed, the ends of it stopped close, and a longitudinal opening made on the side: they beat upon them with two sticks, and the loud and shrill noise these drums give are, in a still evening, heard to a great distance, and are used to spread an alarm: the others are made of light wood, hollowed throughout, and the ends covered with dried goat or sheep skin, laced tight over with cords. Some of these are very large, from six to eight feet long, and two or three feet diameter; in others the heads are only two or three inches apart, and shark's teeth or bits of copper are tied round the rim, which make a jingling noise.

The trombone and tamborine, used in England, appear to have been borrowed from the Africans. They have also two kinds of string instruments; one is a sort of guitar, and is the same as the bangou in the West Indies; the other is in the form of a Welsh harp, but not above two feet long:

long; the ftrings are made of the fibres of a plant and the hair of an elephant's tail.

The women and children alfo have feveral forts of rattles made of gourds, into which they put fmall hard berries; and in Sherbro they have a kind of pipe made of reed, with four ftops for the fingers; and a horn, or trumpet, made of an elephant's tooth.

The cuftomary food of the natives is rice, which they always boil quite dry, and either eat it with palm-oil poured over it, or a ftrong gravy made of fifh, flefh, or fowl, and vegetables boiled together, highly feafoned with pepper and fpices, and palm oil. They ufe very little animal food, and in general prefer it fmoke dried rather than frefh; but are good cooks, and make many favoury difhes.—The men and women always eat apart, and never drink any thing but water at their meals. They eat only twice in the day; the firft time about ten in

the

the morning, and the second about fun-fet; but the principal men who can indulge, generally enjoy a flight repaft early in the morning, which is prepared by the favourite of the preceding night.

The only trades in ufe amongft them are thofe of the carpenter, blackfmith, and griggory maker; and their workmanfhip, confidering the tools they ufe, often difplay neatnefs and ingenuity. Every family fpin and weave their own cloth, and make their own clothes; the men weave and few, and the women fpin and card the cotton. Their drefs is very fimple and eafy. The boys and girls never wear any thing but a *tun-tungeé*, which is a thin flip of cloth paffed between the legs. The different manner of wearing it denotes the fex. The girls have a ftring tied round their waift, and the ends of the *tuntungeé* are tucked under it, and left to hang down before and behind, with a belt or girdle of beads, or loofe

ftrings

ſtrings of them tied round their waiſt; the
boys have the ſhort end forward, the other
part is brought round their loins, tucked
under, and left to hang down behind only.
After marriage the women lay aſide the
tuntungeé, (except among the Nalloes, who
never wear any thing elſe) and wear a cloth
round their waiſt, which reaches down about
the middle of the leg; though they are very
fond of wearing it over their breaſts, not in
order to hide them, but to make them flat,
which (as it is a ſign of womanhood) gives
them additional confequence. They are
alſo very fond of ornaments, ſuch as beads
formed into necklaces, bracelets, &c. ſilver
rings, lockets and chains, manillas, (which
are hoops of ſilver made flat or round to
wear on the wriſts), ſtrings of coral and
uſe a variety of paints. An African lady,
when full dreſt, makes no contemptible
figure :—over her common country cloth,
which we may term her under petticoat,

ſhe

she wears one of red taffity; a black silk
handkerchief tied by two corners round her
neck, hangs down before like a child's bib,
and covers her bosom; another of the same
colour is tied round her head: she has gold
earrings in her ears, round her neck a
string of large coral; and a silver or gold
locket and chain. On each wrist two or
three manillas, and five or six silver rings
on each finger; her forehead is painted
with various angles and triangles of white
or red, and her hair neatly and curiously
plaited; and sometimes close shaved in small
circular or crescent formed spots.—Behind
her follows her waiting-maids, (who are
generally the prettiest girls she can procure,
from ten to fifteen years old), decorated
with coral and beads, and a piece of taffity
or fine chintz thrown over their left
shoulders like a highlander's plaid.

The dress of the men is a loose shirt
without a collar or wristbands, and very
wide

wide sleeves, with drawers which reach
about the middle of the leg, and a hat or
small close cap made of country cloth;
though they generally go bare headed and
bare footed, except the head men, who
imitate as much as they can the dress of
the whites, and the Mandingoes, who are
always distinguished by wearing a red cap
and sandals, and who also ornament their
shirts and drawers with worsted embroi-
dery; in manufacturing of which they are
very ingenious.—The men never go without their belmós, which are large straight
knives, hung in a sheath on the right thigh,
exactly like the patou-patou of the Sand-
wich islands, described by Captain Cook;
they have two of these, one small for the
purpose of eating, and the other as a wea-
pon of defence.

The custom of *tattowing*, or marking the
body, which is called *socoali*, is pretty
general all over Africa, and I fancy was
originally

originally intended to distinguish the different tribes from each other: it is still practised here on that account, but does not appear to be so necessary as it might have been formerly. The back, loins, belly, and breast, are the parts upon which they carve in this neighbourhood; and the manner in which it is done not only denotes the tribe, but the condition of the person, as a slave is not allowed to be marked in the same manner as a free man.—The operation of tattowing must be extremely painful, and is often dangerous; it is performed when the child is only a few months old. Some nations raise the skin in such a manner as to make it appear like embossed work; others perform it by puncture, with a sharp-pointed instrument dipped in a liquid, which leaves an indelible mark: but it must be observed, that those who use this method are of a yellow complexion. In the more southern and eastern parts of

Africa,

Africa, they mark the face as well as the
body.

The fituations which the natives chufe
for their towns are generally on the bank of
a creek or river, for the benefit of fifhing,
and are always diftinguifhed by large pullam
trees; which kind of trees are a certain
criterion of a dry foil. They never take
the trouble to clear more ground than is
fufficient to build their houfes upon; as
they cannot conceive that cutting down the
wood, fo as to admit a free circulation of
air, would render it more healthy : neither
do they obferve any order in the difpofition
of ftreets ; but every man chufing a fpot
moft convenient or agreeable, erects a number of fmall houfes, according to the number
of his wives and people (for every wife has
a feparate houfe); the whole forming a
circle, which are inclofed within a trapada,
or fence, made by driving ftakes into the
ground; which, in a few months, (fo quick

is

is vegetation in this climate) become living trees, and produce a very pretty effect.

A number of these inclosed buildings erected near each other form a town, which is generally surrounded with a mud wall or a strong palisade, and often cover a considerable extent of ground.

When the natives are at war they have several barriers, which are always shut at sun-set, and guarded, during the night, with a good watch; nor are they opened again, upon any occasion, till the sun rises next morning.

Their houses are only one story, and are either round or an oblong square; the sides built with upright posts, wattled and covered with a stiff clay. The floors are also clayed and beat hard; and the roofs are supported with long poles, and thatched with grass. They have generally two doors, on opposite sides, which cause a draught of air through; and, together with their height,

I   make

make them very cool in the hotteſt weather: and they white-waſh the outſide with
white clay, which they get in ſome particular places from the bottom of the river, or a
white ſoapenaceous earth found in Sherbro'.

Though I have mentioned doors, they
very ſeldom have any in the European
manner, except thoſe who imitate the manners of the whites; but, inſtead of doors,
have a mat faſtened to the upper end of
the door frame; when that is dropped
nobody preſumes to enter without a previous
inquiry; when it is rolled up that ceremony
is unneceſſary. The eaves of the roof project ſix or eight feet over the walls, and
are ſupported with poſts; the ſpace between the walls and the poſts is raiſed a
foot or eighteen inches, which form a kind
of piazza, and makes an admirable lolling
place, as it ſcreens them from the ſun
and rain.

In

In the interior parts of the country they build very large houfes of brick baked in the fun, which ftand many years, if the top of the walls are preferved from the weather.

They never nave chimnies to their houfes; yet the natives always keep fires in the morning and evening, to drive away the mufquetos.

The common people, flaves, and children, fleep on mats or dried fkins fpread upon the ground before the fire; but people of confequence have bed places, made by driving four ftakes into the ground, with a bottom of fplit cane or bamboo; and mats hung round fupplies the place of curtains. The men's apartments are furnifhed with a cheft to contain their clothes and valuables, a mat or fkin to fit upon, and their arms. The women's contain al' their domeftic utenfils, mats, and ftools, and never without a looking-glafs.

Near

Near the centre of every town there is a circular building, open at the fides, .which they term a burreé (i. e. court houfe); where all palavers are talked, and public bufinefs of every kind tranfacted.

In the Mandingo country, where they profefs the Mahometan religion, there is in every town a public mofque, from the top of which the people are called to prayers in the fame manner as in Turkey.

There are alfo feveral fmall burreés, which ferve as public fchools; where their youth are taught to read and write Arabic.

Polygamy is allowed and practifed here in its utmoft latitude; and women, as in more civilized countries, are frequently among the great the bond of peace and friendfhip. If two tribes have been at war, or wifh to contract a more clofe and intimate connexion with each other, a mutual exchange with the chiefs of each others daughters is the bafis of every treaty: it

is

is the fame alfo with individuals, and from
this caufe is chiefly the reafon of the head
men having fo many wives. In order to
connect their families together, a female
child is frequently given to a man as foon as
fhe is born; but among the Sufeés the child
remains with the mother till of a proper
age, which is judged of rather from the
external appearance, than from the age of
the party; they are then delivered in form.
On the day appointed for the marriage, the
bridegroom ftations relays of people on the
road the bride is to come, with liquor and
refrefhments; for if thefe articles are not
plentifully fupplied, the bride's attendants
will not proceed a ftep, even though the
fupplies fhould fail them in the midway.
When they approach near the town, they
halt, and are joined by the bridegroom's
people, and friends, who make great rejoicing by fhouting, drinking, firing guns,
and other demonftrations of joy.

I 3   The

The lady is then taken upon the back
of an old woman, and covered over with
a fine cloth, for from this time fhe is not
allowed to be feen by any male perfon, till
after confummation. Mats are fpread on
the ground, that the feet of the perfon who
carries her may not touch the earth; in this
manner fhe   carried to the houfe of her
intended hufband, attended by the friends
of both parties, fhouting dancing, and firing
guns. In the evening the bridegroom retires to his wife's apartment. If he finds
room to fufpect fhe has before admitted the
embraces of a man he immediately leaves
her, which is no fooner known by her
friends than they inftantly abfcond, fhouting and howling with fhame and confufion;
but if he is fatisfied, he remains with her all
night. Great rejoicings are then made by
her friends, who carry the tokens of her vir-
ginity, according to the Mofaical inftitution,
in wild proceffion through the ftreets. In
either

either cafe he is at liberty to retain her, but fhould he fend her back, he muft fend every thing fhe brought with her.

Among the Bullams, Bagoes, and Timmaneys, they frequently receive their future wives when quite children, and bring them up in their own houfes. On thefe occafions, when they receive the child, a prefent is made according to the receiver's ability, to the child's parents, which they term drawing wine for her; but if the child fhould be ill-treated before confummation takes place, her parents have a right to demand her on refunding the wine. On the other hand, if the man fends back his intended bride to her parents, they muft receive her, but keep the wine.

From thefe circumftances one would naturally imagine chaftity was highly valued, but in fact it is no longer the cafe than to the time of marriage; for it is reckoned extremely unpolite and ill-bred for a mar-

I 4   ried

ried woman to reject the offers of a lover;
though she is fenfible she is liable to a fevere punifhment if difcovered, yet it does
not at all affect her *reputation*. Almoft
every married woman has, according to the
country cuftom, her *yangeé cameé*, or cicif-
beo, whom fhe firft folicits. This connexion
fhe is at little or no pains to conceal, and
her hufband is often obliged to be filent,
as otherwife he would have reafon to dread
worfe confequences; for although the laws
of the country are fevere againft adultery,
it requires the arm of power, even among
themfelves, to put them in force. But
it fhould be obferved that it is among
the great who keep a number of wives,
that this practice more particularly pre-
vails. The common people are in general contented with one, or at moft with
two wives. Yet there is one fingular circumftance which fhould not pafs unnoticed
refpecting their women's private amours.—
They

They never attempt to impofe on their hufbands by introducing a fpurious offspring
into his family, but always declare before
they are delivered who is the father. But
if the hufband wifhes to have children by a
favourite woman, he obliges her, though it
is fometimes done voluntarily, to make a
vow, that fhe will not for a certain time go
aftray; and fhould fhe during that period be
induced either by force or perfuafion to break
her vow, fhe immediately tells her hufband,
and both the offending parties undergo a
moft fhameful punifhment, and are ever
after reckoned infamous, and held in con-
tempt.

They depofit their dead in the ground in
the European manner, and generally either
in the evening or morning; but the ceremony of interrogating the corpfe is curious,
and deferves a particular defcription.

When the deceafed is defigned for inter-
ment, the corpfe is laid upon an open bier,
decently

decently wrapped in a white cloth, and born
upon the heads of fix young people, either
male or female; for that is a matter left
entirely to the choice of the corpfe, who
fignifies his approbation or difapprobation of
the bearers, by his inclination or difinclina-
tion to move (which they firmly believe it
is capable of exerting) to the place of
burial. · This place is always in the bufh
out of the town. When arrived there a
perfon, who is generally a relation or friend
of the deceafed, places himfelf five or fix
paces before the bier, with a green bough
in his hand, and addreffes the deceafed in
this manner—" You are now a dead man—
" you know you are no longer alive and as
" one of us—you know you are placed
" upon the fticks (i. e. the bier) of God
" Almighty, and that you muft anfwer
" truth."—And then he afks him what
made him die—whether he knew of his
own death, or whether it was caufed by
witchcraft

witchcraft or poifon; for it is a firm and
univerfal belief among them, that no perfon
dies without having a previous knowledge
of his death, except his death be caufed by
witchcraft or poifon, or the more powerful charms of another perfon over thofe
he wears.

If the corpfe anfwers in the affirmative
to any of the queftions propofed, it is fignified by forcibly impelling the bearers feveral
paces forward, by a power which they fay
they are unable to refift—if, on the contrary,
it is fignified by a rolling motion, which
they alfo fay they cannot prevent.—If, by
the fign given, a fufpicion arifes that the death
of the party was occafioned by poifon or
witchcraft, they proceed to queftion him
who was the perfon, and name feveral
people to whom they fuppofe he was not at-
tached in his life time; but they firft begin
with his relations. If it fhould happen to
be any of them the corpfe remains filent

for

for fome time, as if afhamed to accufe his own kindred, but at laft is obliged to an-fwer. He is then more particularly quef-tioned whether he is certain of the perfon; if he is, it is requefted that he will ftrike that hand which holds the bough, (the perfon before the corpfe holding the bough up in his hand). Upon this the corpfe immediately impels the bier forwards, and ftrikes the bough. In order to convince the fpectators, they repeat this two or three times.

The culprit is then feized, and if a witch fold without further ceremony: and it fre-quently happens if the deceafed were a great man, and the accufed poor, not only he himfelf but his whole family are fold together. But if the death of the de-ceafed was caufed by poifon, the offender is referved for a further trial; from which, though it is in fome meafure voluntary, he feldom efcapes with life.

After depofiting the corpfe in the grave, which is hung round with mats, and his
most

most valued clothes and neceffaries put in with him.—They confine the accufed in fuch a manner that he can releafe himfelf; which fignifies to him he has tranfgreffed the laws of his country, and is no longer at liberty. As foon as it is dark he efcapes to the next town, and there claims the protection of the head man, who is fuppofed to be an impartial perfon; informs him that the corpfe of fuch a perfon has accufed him of caufing his death by poifon; that he is innocent, and defires that to prove it he may drink red water. This requeft is always allowed, and the friends of the deceafed are fent for to be witneffes.

At the time appointed the accufed is placed upon a kind of high chair, ftripped of his common apparel, and a quantity of plantain leaves are wrapped round his waift. Then in prefence of the whole town, who are always affembled upon thefe occafions, he firft eats a little colá or rice, and then drinks the poifoned water. If it kills him,

which

which it is almoft fure to do, he is pronounced guilty; but if he efcapes with
life after drinking five or fix quarts and
throwing up the rice or colá unchanged by
the digeftive powers of the ftomach, he is
judged innocent, but yet not intirely fo till
the fame hour next day. During the in-
terval he is not allowed to eafe nature by
any evacuations; and fhould he not be
able to reftrain them, it would be confidered as ftrong a proof of his guilt as if he
had fallen a victim to the firft draught.
And to prevent the leaft poffibility of the
medicine's not operating, fhould any remain
in the ftomach, they oblige the accufed to
join in the rejoicings made for his efcape,
which confifts in finging and dancing all
night.—After being fairly acquitted by this
ordeal trial, he is held in higher eftimation
than formerly, and brings a palaver, or, to
fpeak in the profeffional language of my
friend, an action againft the friends of the
deceafed,

deceafed, for defamation or falfe imprifonment, which is generally compromifed by a
payment adequate to the fuppofed injury.

But if the deceafed fays he knew of his
death, and that it was premeditated; they
afk him what induced him to die and leave
them, and propofe feveral queftions, fuch
as, was any one poffeffed of a fine gun, or
a fine cloth, that he could not acquire the
fame; or had any body offended him that
he could not be revenged of; but on thefe
accounts they cannot bring any palaver
againft the object of his refentment.

It fometimes happens that the corpfe will
accufe a perfon of caufing his death by
witchcraft, that they cannot fell on account
of their age, or dare not fell on account of
their family or connexions, as it leaves a
ftain upon the family; in that cafe, after the
guilt of the perfon accufed is proved, he
is carried to a field out of the town and
obliged to dig his own grave, the people
who

who are with him as a guard frequently re-
viling him, faying "you deal in death and
can make other people die, you muft now
tafte of it yourfelf." Notwithftanding he goes
on with his work with an appearance of the
utmoft unconcern, retorting, " 'tis true I
did kill fuch a one, and many others, and
if I lived I would kill many more," and
often during his work meafuring the length
and width of the grave, by the dimenfions
of his own body. When the grave is judged
deep enough, they direct the prifoner to
ftand at the edge of the foot of it, with his
face towards it, then a perfon behind ftrikes
him a violent blow upon the nape of the
neck, which caufes him to fall upon his
face into the grave; a little loofe earth is
then thrown upon him, and a fharp ftake
of hard wood is drove through the expiring
delinquent, which pins him to the earth;
the grave is then filled up, and his or her
name is never after mentioned.

Though

Though the ceremonies above related
are conftantly practifed, yet the different
tribes have different methods of performing
them. The Suzeés carry the whole body,
but the Timmaneys and Bullams only the
clothes the deceafed had on at the time of
his death, and the nails of his hands and
feet, which they cut off immediately after
he is expired, and which they hold to have
the fame power to anfwer the queftions
propofed, as if the whole body was prefent,
in which no doubt they are right.

The collufion between the parties concerned in this curious ceremony, is fo ob-
vious, that it appears aftonifhing to me the
common people have not as yet difcovered
it, though it has exifted time immemorial.

I am told that in the interior parts of
the country, they found, fuffering the people to drink red water upon every trifling
occafion, was attended with fuch fatal confequences as would in time depopulate the

K   country;

country; and although they could not intirely fupprefs it, as the common people,
and particularly the women, are ftrongly
prepoffeffed in favour of its infallibility,
they have hit upon a method that has
greatly leffoned the practice.

When a perfon is to drink red water, the
friends of both parties affemble armed as
in a *Polifh diet*, and the inftant the poifon
operates, either in caufing them to vomit or
fall down dead, the friends of the accufed
immediately attack the other party, either
to revenge their injured innocence, or
death.

Though moft unenlightened nations believe in charms and witchcraft, yet the inhabitants of this country are fo much addicted to it that they imagine every thing
is under its influence, and every occurrence
of life they attribute to that caufe; even
the effects of their fometimes diabolical difpofition, they will alledge is owing to the

powers

powers of witches over them; an extraordinary inftance of which has lately happened within my own knowledge. A man of fome confequence, but of a moft vile difpofition, had taken advantage of his fon-in-law's abfence, to commit the moft horrid acts of cruelty on fome of his people; apprehenfive of the confequences on the fon's return, he caufed fome deleterious poifon to be given to one of his daughters; in the agonies which it threw her into, they prevailed on her by promifes of procuring her relief, to confefs fhe had made witch (which is the manner they exprefs it) for her father to fpoil his head, and make him do that bad thing; and he afterwards took care fhe fhould not retract what fhe faid, by giving her a *quietus* in a few days after.

If an allegator deftroys any body when wafhing or fwimming, or a leopard commits depredations on their flocks or poultry; if any perfon is taken fuddenly ill, or dies

fuddenly,

fuddenly, or is feized with any diforder they
are not accuftomed to, it is immediately attributed to witchcraft: and it rarely happens that fome perfon or other is not pointed
out by their conjurors, whom they confult
on thofe occafions, as the witch and fold.

In the power and efficacy of charms,
which they call griggories, they have an
unlimited faith.—Thefe are made of goat's
fkin, either with the hair on, or dreft like
Morocco leather, into various fhapes and
fizes, from the bignefs of a fhilling to the
fize and form of a fheep's heart, and ftuffed
with fome kind of powder, and bits of paper,
on which are written in Arabic fentences
from the Alcoran; thefe they wear tied
round their neck, waift, legs, and arms,
and in fuch numbers that when a man is
properly equipped for the field, the very
weight of them with his gun is an exceeding heavy burthen.

                                        Every

Every griggory is assigned its particular office; one is to preserve him from shot, one from poison, another from fire, others from being drowned; and when a man happens to be killed, burned, or drowned, they only say his griggory was not so good as the person's who occasioned his death; but this must be understood when it happened from an enemy: but they pretend not to any griggory that can preserve them from shot out of great guns and swivels.

They tell many wonderful stories of their griggory men: the relation of one or two of them will set their amazing credulity, in these matters, in a stronger light than any thing else can do.—They tell you their conjurers will go into the water with their hair loose, and continue there half an hour; that they will come up with it perfectly dry, and *plaited* very neatly after the country fashion: that in order to discover theft or adultery they put a quantity of the

K 3   bark

bark of a particular tree into a small country earthen pot; this they fill full of water,
and put upon the fire: after it has boiled
some time, the conjurer drops a small stone
into it, which he takes out two or three
times with his hand, to convince the specta-
tors that he feels no inconvenience from the
heat of the water. ˉHe then orders the
culprit to take the stone out; if he is innocent the water will not burn him; if it does
he is guilty; which is generally the case
when any female culprits are tried for
adultery.

Another method, *equally efficacious* as the
former, is done as follows:—The conjurer
fills a pewter bason, or brass pan, full of
water; then sets up a stick on each side;
from the tops of the sticks he stretches a
small cord, and from the center of that
cord suspends a grain of pepper by a thread,
just to touch, but not in the water; he
then dips his fingers in the water and flirts
them

them in the culprit's face; if he is guilty a white film immediately covers his eyes, which deprives him of fight and caufes moft excruciating pain; but, if he is innocent, it has no effect. After the guilty party has made his confeffion the conjurer dips his fingers into the fame water, and fprinkles a little in his face, which inftantly relieves him from pain and reftores him to fight.—Thefe things are always done in open day, and before a concourfe of people; and what is moft extraordinary, it may be performed by proxy. The conjurers alfo pretend to foretell future events by cafting fand or ftones into the air.

A capital white trader, who has refided near thirty years upon the coaft, and who is otherwife a man of fenfe, told me, very ferioufly, he once thought as he fuppofed I did; but that he had feen fo many furprifing inftances of their art he could no longer doubt.

K 4　　　　　　　in

In the accounts of moſt uncivilized countries that we read of, we find the office of phyſician is generally annexed to that of prieſt or conjurer; but here it is carried on by old women, and the cures they perform are truly aſtoniſhing; particularly in external wounds, by the uſe of ſimples, which their woods and fields afford in abundance:

The diſeaſes they are moſt ſubject to are intermitting fevers and the hydrocele; the latter is ſuppoſed to be cauſed by the too frequent uſe of palm wine, and exceſs of venery. The venereal diſeaſe is frequent, but never attended with thoſe dreadful ſymptoms which too often accompany it in Europe, and is always eaſily cured; neither can they be convinced that it proceeds from impure coition. The ſmall-pox is endemial, but is not ſo frequent on the ſea-coaſt as in the interior country.

I ſhall

I fhall conclude with my beft wifhes for your health and happinefs; ·

And believe me,

DEAR SIR,

Your's truly.

LETTER VII.

Sierra-Leone, February 15, 1787.

DEAR SIR,

YOUR laft letter reached me, I prefume, much fooner than you would expect, as it was only five weeks from the date in coming to Africa. Your pointing out to me thofe fubjects concerning which you wifh to be informed, is a pleafing and convincing proof of your confidence and efteem.

teem. I shall make this letter the best an-
swer I am able to your first inquiry, namely,
the present state and manner of the African
trade.

The Portuguese were the original disco-
verers of the whole coast of Africa, and
most of the trading places still retain the
names given them by the first adventurers;
they also formed many considerable settlements, vestiges of which are still remaining, not more remarkable for the durability
of the materials with which they were constructed, than the excellence of the situa-
tions, which no doubt were then, and still
are, the best that could possibly be fixed
upon for trade; but the only settlements
they now have on the coast of Africa are,
Loanga St. Paul's, and Baffou, and a small
fort at Whydah; from the former, which
is their principal settlement, they send a
great number of slaves to the Brasils.

In

In the infancy of the African trade, gold, ivory, wax, gums, oftrich feathers, and feveral fpecies of medicinal, and dye woods, conftituted what might then be termed the ftaple commodities of the country, and which were purchafed from the natives with glafs beads, coarfe woollen cloths, brandy; and and fundry coarfe and cheap ornaments of brafs or iron. Nor was it 'till the Europeans had formed fettlements in the Weft Indies, that flaves became an article of traffick.

In proportion as the Weft Indies were cultivated, the demand for flaves increafed, as they were found to anfwer for that purpofe much better than Europeans, and were alfo procured at a much eafier expence. The Englifh and French were the firft who began to cultivate the windward iflands, which had been only vifited by the Spaniards, their firft difcoverers, and in confequence

quence were the firft who entered into
competition with the Portuguefe in the African trade. The fubfequent wars of that
nation with the Dutch, and other European
ftates becoming adventurers alfo, foon dif-
poffeffed them of the greateft part of it;
but this competition intirely changed the
nature of the trade; the natives foon availed
themfelves of the eagernefs and avidity,
with which each adventurer ftrove to out-
vie the other, and their demands increafed
accordingly. Slaves as well as the other
productions of the country, which were formerly purchafed with a few cheap and fimple articles, were not now to be bought
without a more extenfive and valuable af-
fortment of cloths, fire arms, powder, fhot,
great variety of beads, and filver ware: and
foon after this trade was regulated in much
the fame manner in which it is carried on
at prefent.—Cuftom has authorized what
fancy began; in affigning to almoft every
　　　　　　　　　　　　　　　　　feparate

feparate diftrict in Africa a different choice
of goods, particularly in their arms, beads,
and cloth, and in affixing different denominations of value to the articles of trade.
From Senegal to Cape Mount the name of
the nominal value given to goods is called
bars, from which it is denominated the bar
trade; from Cape Mount to Cape Palmas
they are called pieces, and therefore the
piece trade; from Cape Palmas all along
the Gold Coaft to Whydah, they are
termed Ackeys; from thence to Benin
Pawns; and from Benin to Bonny, New
and Old Calabar, Camaroons, and Gaboon,
Coppers.

It may be prefumed that the fea-coaft
alone at firft furnifhed the flaves which
were fold to the Europeans; but the conftant and increafing demand, which has
unremittingly continued from the firft time of
their being brought to America, foon obliged
the natives to have recourfe to the back
country;

country; and many of them are now brought from a very great diftance.

The modes of dealing and procuring flaves are in moft places extremely different; but, as I cannot pretend to defcribe them all, I fhall confine myfelf to a defcription of the method of trade of thefe parts only.

When the adventurer arrives upon the coaft with a fuitable cargo—w¹ ˙ this place confifts of European and ..uian cotton and linen goods, filk ha· ·chicfs, taffities, coarfe blue and red woollen cloths, fcarlet cloth in grain, coarfe and fine hats, worfted caps, guns, powder, fhot, fabres, lead bars, iron bars, pewter bafons, copper kettles and pans, iron pots, hardware of various kinds, earthen and glafs ware, hair and gilt leather trunks, beads of various kinds, filver and gold rings and ornaments, paper, coarfe and fine check, and linen ruffled fhirts and caps, Britifh and foreign fpirits and tobacco —

he

he difpatches his boats properly equipped to the different rivers On their arrival at the place of trade they immediately apply to the head man of the town, inform him of their bufinefs, and requeft his protection; defiring he will either be himfelf their landlord, or appoint a refpectable perfon, who becomes fecurity for the perfon and goods of the ftranger, and alfo for the recovery of all money lent, provided it is done with his knowledge and approbation. This bufinefs finifhed, and proper prefents made, (for nothing is done without) they proceed to trade either by lending their goods to the natives, who carry them up into the country, or by waiting till trade is brought to them.—The former is the moft expeditious way, when they fall into good hands; but the latter is always the fafeft.

When the country people come down themfelves to trade with the whites, they are obliged to apply to the inhabitants of

the

the villages where the factories are kept, to ferve as brokers and interpreters.

When a flave is brought to be fold he is firft carefully examined, to fee that there is no blemifh or defect in him; if approved, you then agree upon the price at fo many bars, and give the dealer fo many flints or ftones to count with; the goods are therf delivered to him piece by piece, for which he returns fo many ftones for each, agreeably to its denominated value; and they always take care to begin with thofe articles which they judge moft effentially neceffary.

Exclufive of this method of dealing directly with the natives, tranfient fhips, or thofe who only come for a fmall number, generally barter with the white traders refident on the coaft, or with the factories eftablifhed there, who take their whole cargo at once, and deliver them flaves,

camwood,

camwood, ivory, &c. according to their
agreement, in a certain time.

From the great number of flaves which
are annually exported, and which, from this
place and the parts adjacent, including
Sherbro' and the Riomoonas, amounts to
about three thoufand annually, one would
be led to imagine the country would, in
time, be depopulated; inftead of which no
diminution of their numbers is perceived;
and, from every account we have been able
to acquire from the natives themfelves, who
travel into the interior country, it is ex-
traordinarily populous: but how fuch a
number of flaves are procured, is a circumftance which I believe no European was
ever fully acquainted with.

The beft information I have been able
to collect is, that great numbers are prifoners taken in war, and are brought down,
fifty or a hundred together, by the black
flave merchants; that many are fold for

L   witchcraft,

witchcraft, and other real, or imputed, crimes; and are purchased in the country with European goods and salt; which is an article so highly valued, and so eagerly fought after, by the natives, that they will part with their wives and children, and every thing dear to them, to obtain it, when they have not slaves to dispose of; and it always makes a part of the merchandize for the purchase of slaves in the interior country; yet, notwithstanding salt is in such great demand, the natives of the sea-coast will not permit the import of it in European vessels, because it would inter-fere with the only article of their own manufacture, which they have for inland trade.

The present custom and ancient tradition of the country, handed down from father to son, and from generation to generation, both teach us to believe that the practice of making, buying, and selling slaves, was in

ufe

ufe in Africa long before our knowledge of
it. Death or flavery were, and ftill are,
the punifhments for almoft every offence.
And every prifoner taken in battle was
either put to death or kept as a flave.
The fate of prifoners was alfo in a great
meafure determined by the feafon of the
year, and the occafion they had for their
fervices. If they were taken after the harveft was over, they were feldom fpared; but
thofe who were captured before the commencement of the rice feafon, experienced
a different fate, as they were referved to cultivate the rice-ground; and fold, after the
harveft, to thofe tribes bordering on the fea,
who had no other means of acquiring flaves
than by purchafe; or were kept as labouring flaves, and for ever fixed to the fpot.
This was the ancient cuftom of the country,
and the modern practice is nearly fimilar,
as they feldom difpofe of their new flaves
till the rice is in the ground, or until it is

cut.

cut. Hence, though the Europeans by the eagerneſs with which they puſh this trade may be cenſurable ſo far, as they may ſome times, by their competition with each other, excite the avarice of individuals to procure ſlaves, by means as repugnant to their own laws as any act of diſhoneſty is to ours; yet I believe we may ſafely conclude, that ſlavery can never be aboliſhed in a country like Africa, conſiſting of a prodigious number of ſmall independent ſtates, perpetually at variance, and under no reſtraining form of government, where the people are of a vindictive and revengeful ſpirit, and where the laws make every man a ſlave who is convicted of the moſt trifling offence. During the late war in which England was engaged with France, when the ſhips did not viſit the coaſt as uſual, and there were no goods to purchaſe the ſlaves which were brought down, the black merchants ſuffered many of them to periſh for want of food,

food, and faid they fhould not come down again till the fhips arrived. When queftioned what the inland people would do with their flaves? they replied " cut their throats, as they ufed to do before white men came to their country." And I am credibly informed, however fhocking to relate, that this was, during that period, the cafe with great numbers. To the above account it may be neceffary to add a fhort defcription of the prefent ftate of flavery in Africa.

Among the Suzeés, Bullams, Bagoes, and Timmaneys, three fourths at leaft of the inhabitants are flaves; and among the Mandingoes a much larger proportion.—It is not an unufual thing for a head man to have two or three hundred flaves of both fexes, exclufive of their domeftics who are very numerous; and fome of the principal men among the Mandingoes have from feven hundred to

L 3   a thoufand,

a thoufand, who refide together diftinct
from their mafters, in what they call their
flave towns;—thefe people know and feel
their fituation, for they are employed in
ever fervile and laborious occupation; but
there is a diftinction to be made between
the labouring and the houfe flave, the former is as it were fixed to the foil, and held
in no higher eftimation than any other animal that contributes to its cultivation ; but
the latter is in fome refpect confidered as a
branch of the family, affumes his mafter's
name, and calls him father; yet thefe are
hired out as failors or labourers, not only
to the Europeans, who are fettled, or come
to trade there, but alfo to each other; and
their mafters receive the wages of their
labour. They are alfo obliged to attend their
mafters in their wars and predatory excur-
fions, and frequently experience a change
of them from that caufe.—It is related of
the North American Indians, that when

any

any of them are taken in battle, and refcued from death, by being adopted into a family, they immediately confider themfelves as a part of that tribe into whofe hands they are fallen, and would the next day march to attack their former friends with as much zeal as if they had never known them, but had been brought up amongſt their new connexions.

The conduct of the African flave when taken in battle, or fold to another maſter, is nearly fimilar, as inſtances are extremely rare of flaves deferting the fervice of a pre-fent to return to that of a former owner, (except in cafes of extreme ill ufage). Born a flave he knows no other fituation; and it is alike indifferent to him, whether he be the property of this or that man, as long as he is provided with the neceffaries of life.

It is not to be doubted but the ideas of a flave, when fold to one of his own country and colour, and when fold to an European,

L 4 are

are extremely different. In the firſt inſtance
his ſituation, and the cuſtom of his country,
ſoon reconcile him to the change; but in
the latter caſe, he imagines the white man
buys him either to offer him as a ſacrifice
to his God, or to devour him as food; and I
have ſeen ſome of theſe poor wretched
beings ſo terrified with apprehenſions of
their expected fate, as to remain in a ſtate
of torpid inſenſibility for ſome time, till, by
kind treatment, and making them under-
ſtand for what uſes they were purchaſed,
the impreſſions of fear were gradually leſ-
ſoned; others have obſtinately refuſed their
food, while ſome of a bolder conſtitution
have looked at a white man with amaze-
ment, but without fear, examined his ſkin
and their own, opened his breaſt, and felt
whether the hair on his head was faſt, or
not, and frequently burſt into laughter at
the contraſt, and, to him no doubt, uncouth
appearance of a white man.

To

To reafon from ones own fentiments, we fhould be led to fuppofe that thofe attachments which muft in every fituation necefarily fubfift between the fexes, where they are together, would make them regret a feparation; but the facility with which they form new connexions, and the knowledge that their children are the properties of their mafters, foon remove all anxiety on thefe occafions.

Yet notwithftanding the almoft abfolute power which the mafter has over the life and property of his flave, he cannot fell any who are born his flaves, or who, though purchafed, have refided twelve months in his poffeffion, without accufing them of fome crime; but for an accufation they are never at a lofs.

Witchcraft is the moft general charge; and fuch is the aftonifhing folly and fuperftition of thefe people, whether a flave or freeman, that they generally acknowledge

themfelves

themſelves guilty of the crime of which they are accuſed; but if a ſlave ſhould plead not guilty, it would little avail him, as, on theſe occaſions, the maſter is both the accuſer and judge; and, if a free- man, he would be obliged to drink red water, which is a poiſoned liquor prepared on the occaſion. The analogy between this mode of trial and thoſe which formerly obtained in England is very ſtriking.

The Mandingoes, who are extremely cruel in the treatment of their ſlaves, had carried this practice to ſuch an exceſs, that, in 1785, there was a general inſurrection. The ſlaves took an opportunity, when the principal part of their fighting men were out upon an expedition, to attack their maſters; ſeveral of whom they put to death, and had their heads carried before them on poles, as enſigns of victory and liberty; they then ſet fire to the rice which was ready to be cut, which reduced the Man-

dingoes

dingoes to the utmoft diftrefs, who afterwards retreated to their towns, which they
fortified in fuch a manner, and fo effectu-
ally ftopped every avenue that led into the
country from whence the Mandingoes could,
receive affiftance, that their late haughty
mafters were under the neceffity of fuing
for peace—whether they will return again
to their former obedience, or affert their
independence, is yet undecided.

Another method which they make ufe
of to difpofe of their flaves is, to put them
in pawn either to the fhips and factories, or
the native traders, for a limited time; and
if they are not redeemed at the expiration
of that time, they become flaves to the
perfon to whom they were pawned; but
fhould a pawn be fent off before the
time is expired, or even after, without
giving notice to the perfon who pawned,
him, a palaver, or action, would be brought
againft the perfon fo offending.

It

It is cuſtomary, indeed, for people of all
ranks to put their children out as pledges, but
then they are careful either to redeem
them in time or to pawn them to the re-
ſident traders or eſtabliſhed factories; and
theſe pawns are generally conſidered as a
protection for your property, and are employed in all domeſtic offices; but are
equally liable to be ſent off, if not redeemed in due time, as the pawned ſlave.
And it ſhould alſo be obſerved, that a
perſon, whether a ſlave or the ſon of a
freeman, if not redeemed at the expiration of the time limited for his redemption,
becomes ſo much the abſolute property of
the perſon to whom he was pawned, that,
ſhould he be kept in the country for the purpoſe of a domeſtic, yet it is intirely at the
option of his maſter whether he will ever after
let him be redeemed, though they ſhould offer
twenty for one, or he ſhould be a ſon of the
moſt powerful perſon in the country.

From

From the public papers you were so obliging to fend me, I find much has been faid on the fubject of the African trade; particularly refpecting the inhumanity of it; I muft confefs I do not fee it in that light; and when you have attentively confidered the particulars which I have related, I flatter myfelf you will join me in opinion. — A pretty clofe parallel may be obferved between the African condemned for fome offence againft the laws of his country, to be fold to a white man, and the Englifh felon tranfported to a wild uncultivated country; for fuch Botany Bay is reprefented, and whofe diftance for ever excludes the hope of returning.

Every circumftance of grief or diftrefs which can increafe the affliction of the African at parting from his native country, very probably may be felt with redoubled force by the more enlightened European.

It

It might be urged in fupport of this commerce, that the cruelty of the laws in
Africa, which punifh with death, is miti-
gated by tranfportation, as flavery would
undoubtedly be the portion of thefe unhappy people in their native country. This
is unalterable; but if their fituation in our
Weft India iflands is fuch as could be reftored by wife and humane regulations,
fuch a plan would redound much to the
honour of the Britifh legiflature, and may
be confidered as the only effectual relief
that, under the prefent circumftances of
Africa, can be adminiftered.

I know it is urged by writers on this
fubject, that all mankind are by nature free
and equal, and that no one has a right to
fubjugate the perfon of another to flavery.

In the writings, however, of many religious and moral philofophers, it is con-
tended, that though man, of created beings,

holds

holds the firſt link, yet that there are different degrees of excellence in the human race, as there are in every other animal, or deſcending link, of the great chain of nature.

In Africa experience fully authorizes our aſſent to this :—Trace the manners of the natives, the whole extent of Africa from Cape Cantin to the Cape of Good Hope, and you find a conſtant and almoſt regular gradation in the ſcale of underſtanding, till the wretched Cafre ſinks nearly below the Ouran Outang.

LETTER

LETTER VIII.

Liverpool, Feb. 20, 1788.

DEAR SIR,

WHEN a fubject of great national importance is agitated, and the minds of men
are much divided, it is undoubtedly the
duty of every good citizen to communicate
every kind of information to the public
which his obfervation and experience may
furnifh. Upon this principle, therefore, and
in compliance with your requeft, I fhall endeavour, in as concife and as perfpicuous a
manner as I can, to ftate thofe facts which
I have collected from my refidence at Sierra-
Leone, in Africa, and to fuggeft fuch obfervations,

vations, as appear particularly to concern the African flave trade.

To thofe who contend that this commerce fhould be reprobated as entirely repugnant to moral law and the gofpel, this anfwer might perhaps be given—that there are, and neceffarily muft be, many inftitutions, confidering the depravity of human nature, and the ftate of fociety in general, equally incompatible with morality and Chriftianity. It might likewife be added that, perhaps for wife reafons infcrutable to us, this fyftem and others analagous to it may be tolerated by Providence. To thofe who infift that no part of mankind hath any right to opprefs, captivate, or wage war upon any other part, for any purpofes of dominion or intereft, might it not be obferved, that men are by nature equal, and confequently that in church and ftate there fhould be no fubordination? thefe two pofitions, or fpeculative truths cannot be denied. The

M   theory

theory is admired by the philanthropift, but the practice, being attended with infuperable difficulties, is rejected by the politician.

Self prefervation makes it occafionally neceffary to have recourfe to arms, and to attack a rival nation without any apparent provocation; and, for the good order of fociety, there muft be gradations of rank, and a fcale of political dependance.

I have been forry to remark, that perfons who have delivered their fentiments againft the abolition of this trade, have been branded with the name of hirelings of flavery, and other opprobrious epithets. There are no *arguments* in *abufe*; and as I addrefs myfelf only to perfons of enlarged and liberal minds, I have nothing of that fort to apprehend. I fhall therefore proceed by obferving, that the fcope of this letter will be confined to the mode of *procuring flaves* on the coaft of Africa, and to the impolicy of

abolifhing

abolifhing a traffic of fuch effential importance to the naval interefts of Great Britain.

A defcription of the method of procuring flaves in the part of Africa where I refided, I have, in fome meafure, anticipated
in my former letters from Sierra-Leone,
which were written at a time when I had
no idea of a defign to abolifh that trade being formed, or I fhould have applied myfelf with greater induftry to have acquired
a more particular knowledge of the manners
and cuftoms of the natives. of the interior
countries; I fhall however endeavour to
combat fuch affertions as are made ufe
of by the advocates for the abolition of this
commerce, as my own knowledge and information may fuggeft. That flaves are
often captives taken in war, is a pofition I
readily accede to; but that thofe wars are
undertaken merely for the purpofe of procuring flaves is by no means the cafe; for
it is neceffary to obferve, the king, or chief

M 2   of

of a tribe, has not power to make war upon
any other tribe without the confent and
approbation of the principal people of his
nation; and it can fcarcely be conceived that
fuch confent could be obtained to a meafure
that would draw down upon them the refentment of the neighbouring ftates. Neither is it (as is alledged) in any inftance
which has occurred to my obfervation or
inquiries, by the inftigation of the European
traders; for, whenever the people on the
fea-coaft are at war, it puts an entire ftop
to trade; and I always found it my intereft,
as well as my inclination, to reconcile their
differences, and to preferve peace. But
furely no perfon can ferioufly imagine that
the Africans are without paffions, or that
their difpofitions are fo placid, as to be un-
moved by anger or refentment, and excited
to action by avarice alone. In my former
letters I have defcribed the caufes of the
wars that fubfifted in the countries about

Sierra-

Sierra-Leone when I arrived there; and I believe I may with confidence affert, that fuch caufes are generally the origin of their quarrels.

In anfwer to the charge of kidnapping flaves, I can only fay that I never heard of fuch a practice, nor do I know a word in their language expreffive of fuch a cuftom ever having had exiftence.

Thofe who vifit Africa in a curfory manner have few opportunities of acquiring any intimate knowledge of the country or its inhabitants, and are very liable to be miftaken in the meaning of the natives, from want of knowledge in their language, or in the jargon of fuch of them as refide upon the fea-coaft and fpeak a little Englifh; the European affixing the fame ideas to the words fpoken by the African, as if they were pronounced by one of his own nation.

M 3   A fpecimen

A specimen of the conversation which generally passes on these occasions will elucidate this observation. " *Well, my friend,* " *you got trade to day; you got plenty of* " *slaves?*" " *No, we no got trade yet; by and* " *by trade come, you can't go.* *" " *What, you* " *go for catch people, you go for make war?*" " *Yes, my brother, or my friend, gone for* " *catch people; or they gone for make war.*"

By this conversation nothing more is meant by the African than that his brother, or his friend, was gone into the country to purchase slaves from the nations who are at war; or, perhaps, his own tribe might be at war with some of the neighbouring states; and as they in general sell their prisoners, (though even now it is not always the case, revenge sometimes proving too powerful for avarice) they may wish the ship to remain in expectation of having more prisoners to dispose of. But I must again

---

* By which they mean to signify their desire for the ship to stay,

repeat

repeat that the primary caufe of thefe wars is not merely to procure flaves, but arifes from the captious, quarrelfome, and vindictive, difpofition of the people. But it is not the prifoners made in the wars which the inhabitants of the fea-coaft have with each other, nor thofe whom the laws' of their country, in confequence of their crimes, punifh with flavery, that conftitute a tenth part of the flaves who are purchafed by the Europeans; for, in fact, the inhabitants of the fea-coaft are only the merchants and brokers, and carry the goods which they receive from the Europeans into the interior country, and there purchafe the flaves from other merchants.

The nations who inhabit the interior parts of Africa, eaft of Sierra-Leone, profefs the Mahometan religion; and, following the means prefcribed by their prophet, are perpetually at war with the furrounding nations who refufe to embrace their religi-

ous

ous doctrines (and I have before shewn the zeal with which the Mandingoes inculcate their faith).

The prisoners made in these religious wars furnish a great part of the slaves which are sold to the Europeans; and would, I have reason to believe, from the concurring testimony of many of the most intelligent natives, be put to death if they had not the means of disposing of them.

That death would be the fate of their prisoners, the example of the inhabitants of Madagascar, is sufficient proof; for since the Portuguese have declined dealing with them they put all their prisoners to death. *

It is also given as a reason for the abolishing this traffic; that the distinctions of crimes are multiplied, and every transgres-

* The circumstance of the king of Dahomy putting his prisoners to death which he took in the Whydah war, has been made known to the privy council by an eye-witness.

sion

fion punifhed with flavery, in confequence
of their intercourfe with Europeans.

Upon this head I fhall obferve, that the
crimes of murder, poifon, witchcraft, adultery, and theft, are always confidered as
capital, and have been punifhed with either
death or flavery from time immemorial.

That the punifhment of death, for the
commiffion of thefe crimes, is remitted by
their becoming flaves, I believe, in many inftances, to be the cafe; yet, furely no one
would adduce this circumftance as a proof
of its inhumanity. Leffer offences, whether they refpect the religious ceremonies,
or particular cuftoms of the country, are
punifhed by fine; which, if the defendant
is not able to pay, he becomes the flave of
the plaintiff till redeemed : nor can he be
redeemed without the profecutor's confent.

Such are, and fuch always have been,
from every information I could collect, the
laws and cuftoms of the natives of Africa

at

at and about Sierra-Leone. Indeed it has greatly aftonifhed me to find that the long intercoufe they have had with Europeans, and particularly with the Englifh, fhould have fo little affected their manners and cuftoms. Several white men, natives of Great Britain, are now refident in the country, who have remained there upwards of twenty years; but the African born children fpeak no other language than their mothers, and in every refpect follow the cuftoms of the country: and what appears to me as a ftrong proof of the little incli-nation they have hitherto fhewn to profit by the knowledge of European arts is, that thofe black and Mulatto children (and there are not a few of them) who are fent to Europe for their education *, on their

* The natives of Africa, in moft parts where the Englifh trade, are defirous of fending their children to England to learn what they call white man's book;

their return to their native country immediately reaffume the manner of living, and
embrace the fuperftitious cuftoms and ceremonies of their countrymen.   The only
apparent influence it has upon them is in
the exterior decoration of their perfons, and
the interior ornaments of their houfes.

I have, in my letters before alluded to,
defcribed the ftate of flavery in Africa, and
here it may not be confidered as irrelevant

book; a knowledge which they find neceffary for
carrying on their trade.   There are always feveral
of thefe children in Liverpool, who are boarded and
educated by the merchants and mafters of fhips
trading to Africa.

Query. Might not this plan of educating the
African children in England, and inftructing them
in the principles of the Chriftian religion, be a more
likely mean f civilizing and converting the natives
to Chriftianity, than a fupenfion or abolition of our
trade with them; which would for ever leave them
involved in the dark errors of paganifm, or to become
converts to the difciples of Mahomet?   j

                                                    to

to the fubject to fay a few words on the
treatment of them in that country.   The
labouring flaves go to work before the fun
rifes, and continue in the field or wood * till
ten o'clock, about which time they take
their repaft, and I believe do not exceed an
hour before they return again to their labour, which continues till fun-fet.   Their
manner of punifhing the labouring flave is
fevere—the offender is ftretched upon the
earth with his face downward, and is either
held in that pofition by men, or faftened to
four ftakes drove into the ground, and is
beaten with rods as thick as a man's finger,
at the will of his mafter.   The Mandingoes,
according to a precept of the Alcoran, limit
the number of ftripes to be inflicted for
fmall crimes to forty lacking one, and for

---

* The cutting down woods for the purpofe of
making rice plantations in Africa, is a much more
laborious employment than the cultivation of fugar
or cotton in the Weft Indies.

greater

greater offences to ninety and nine; but few furvive the greater punifhment. They alfo punifh by confining the feet in wooden ftocks, which, though not fixed, are too heavy to be removed by any perfon confined in them.—Whether the condition of a flave in Africa or the Weft Indies is materially different, I muft, from the circumftances I have ftated, leave the public to determine*. The freeman indeed who has felt and enjoyed the fweets of liberty, to him the deprivation of it, though condemned by the laws of his country, or the fate of war, muft no doubt be painful: but the man who is born a flave, who feels no alteration in his circumftances from a change of mafters, and who never even in idea felt the fenti-

* The flaves who are employed by the white people refident in Africa as domeftics and failors, find their fituation fo materially different from ferving their black mafters, that inftances of defertion are very rare.

ments

ments which liberty alone can infpire, as
he fuffers not by the comparifon, fo he is
not fo great an objeȼt of our commiferation.
But what have we to do with the African
laws; may not the rulers in that country
infliȼt what punifhments they think proper,
they are not our fubjeȼts, neither are they
ever likely to become fo? The genius of the
people, and of that religion, which will in
all probability one day prevail throughout
that extenfive continent, are equally averfe
to the introduȼtion of European manners
or European laws.

But let us fuppofe that the flave trade
was abolifhed by every nation in Europe,
would it abolifh it in Africa, or would it in
any meafure add to the happinefs of the natives of that country? That it would not
abolifh it in Africa is an incontrovertible
truth to thofe who are at all acquainted
with the ftate of the interior country, or
the commerce that is there carried on.

The

The troops of the emperor of Morocco
are compofed of black flaves purchafed in
the more fouthern parts of Africa: and it is
not unlikely that other defpotic princes, both
in the fouth and eaft parts, may compofe
their armies in the fame manner; and I am
credibly informed that in the northern and
eaftern parts of Africa the flave trade is
carried on in large caravans of two or three
thoufand flaves and people travelling together, and are difperfed over every part of
Turkey, Perfia, and Arabia: but, independent of the numbers exported out of the
country, either from the weftern or other
parts of the continent, by the Arab or by the
European, there is an internal traffic amongft
the natives.

Slaves are the medium, inftead of coin,
for the purchafe of every neceffary, and the
fupplying of every want; and every article
is eftimated, by its proportion, to the value
of a flave. I need not point out to the
intelligent

intelligent reader the analogy between this custom and that of all countries where coin is not used, or where it is a scarce article; nor is it very material whether a guinea, a sheep, cow, or a slave, are the denominations of value.

But would the abolition of this trade add to the happiness of the natives of Africa? I conceive not; and for the same reason that would attend the abolition of the trade of this kingdom to foreign parts.—For what purpose do we carry on a trade with the East Indies and other foreign places, but to supply us with the luxuries (not the neceffaries) of life? Of the latter our own country affords us abundance; but were we deprived of the former, we should, from being accustomed to consider them as contributing to our happiness, severely feel the want of them.

The African is placed in the same situation, by his commerce with the Europeans,

in

in such productions as his country affords,
and which to him were no new article of
traffic; he is enabled to acquire not only the
neceffaries, but fuch articles alfo as add to
the enjoyment of life; and in the poffeffion
of which he places no inconfiderable fhare
of his happinefs.

On the impolicy of abolifhing the African
flave trade I fhall beg leave to offer a few obfervations, and to point out the moft probable confequences of fuch a determination.

The French, in the year 1784, in order
to encourage the African flave trade, granted
a bounty of forty fhillings per ton upon
every veffel employed in that trade, and
a further bounty of near eight pounds fter-
ling upon every flave imported into certain
parts of their Weft India iflands.

This bounty has already enabled them to
monopolize the whole trade of the coaft of
Angola, and to fhare equally with the Englifh
at Bonny and other places ; and has confe-

N   quently

quently caufed an increafe of their fhipping and feamen, and a decreafe of ours in the fame proportion.

If we thus fuffer a diminution in the number of fhips and feamen employed in this trade from competition only, what muft be the confequence fhould an abolition of the trade itfelf take place, I leave to every unprejudiced reader to determine.

But it is not the lofs of the fhips and men employed in the flave trade only that would leffen our maritime ftrength, the Weft India trade alfo would foon be annihilated; for whatever vifionary fchemes may be propofed for fupplies of people to cultivate the fugar iflands, experience, the moft unerring guide, has fufficiently proved that no Europeans can ftand the climate when employed in the cultivation of the foil *.

---

* Independent of the expence, as no white man can be hired under one dollar per day.

But

But this is not the extent of the political evil which may arife, not only from a total abolition of the African trade, but is even to be dreaded, fhould any partial or injudicious reftrictions be laid upon it.

Whenever any particular branch of commerce becomes no longer profitable to the parties concerned in carrying it on, either from reftraints upon the trade itfelf, or want of encouragement from the government to enable them to meet the competition of rival ftates, or from whatever caufe it may proceed, that trade will confequently either totally fubfide, or fink into infignificance: and if it be of fuch a nature that the inftruments by which it was carried on cannot be employed in any other way, from a fufficient number being already in ufe; and if, at the fame time, rival ftates are ufing every means to poffefs thofe inftruments, in order to increafe and extend that particular branch of trade, is it not to be apprehended that

N 2   the

the proprietor of fuch inftruments would difpofe of, or employ them, where he alone could do it to advantage?

The merchant, his fortune, experience, factor's fhips, and the feamen employed in them, are the inftruments by which the African and all other foreign trades are carried on: and there cannot be a doubt, but that thofe merchants who have employed their fortunes in this trade, under the fanction and authority of the legiflature of their country, would (fhould they be deprived of it either *in toto* or under any reftrictions which would render it unprofitable,) immediately remove, with every confequent contingent, to that country where they could find encouragement. And it may not be unneceffary to mention that France and Spain are at this moment, and indeed long have been, holding out every inducement to the Britifh merchants and feamen, experienced in the African bufinefs, to

enter

enter into their fervice. Confidering it in this point of view, it appears a meafure fraught with the moft alarming tendency to the naval intereft of thefe kingdoms, and pregnant with fuch confequences (as would inevitably refult from it) as cannot have been duly reflected upon by the warmeft of its advocates.

It is not for the intereft of the individuals only who are concerned in the African trade that I contend, it is for the welfare of the nation at large; for it is a truth that needs no illuftration, that, for every fhip withdrawn from this trade by the Englifh, France or Spain would have an additional one, as the idea of abolifhing it has never yet, I believe, been thought of in the cabinets of Verfailles or Madrid.

The confequences which might enfue upon the abolition of the flave trade to the merchants trading to the Weft Indies, and the proprietors of the Sugar Iflands; the influence

fluence it would have upon the trade of the
Eaft India Company,* and the manufac-
turers of this country, I muft leave to thofe
who are better informed to lay before the
public; but to thofe whofe objections againft
the African trade arife from the fuppofed
inhumanity of it, I muft beg leave to fuggeft
a few particulars.

It is, I believe, a generally received opinion, that a nation without foreign wars,
colonies, or foreign traffic, double it's
numbers in the fpace of thirty or forty
years; admitting this to be the cafe, when
a country becomes over ftocked with inhabitants whom they cannot employ, how are
they to difpofe of their fuperfluous numbers.
They muft either follow the example of
the Chinefe, and drown the fupernumerary
infants as foon as born, or they will enact
fanguinary laws, which punifh alike with
death the prifoner of war and the perpe-

* Eaft India cotton, and fome filk goods, compofe a part of every African cargo.

trator

trator of crimes. To mitigate the punish-
ment of death by slavery or banishment, is
a proof of civilization operating in favour of
humanity; and every circumstance which
contributes to that end, should undoubtedly
be attributed to the same cause.

The trade therefore which the Europeans
carry on with the natives of Africa for
slaves, is probably permitted by Providence
as a means of preserving the lives of the
many thousands who would otherwise be
put to death, and are thus made useful
members of society.

THE END.

www.ingramcontent.com/pod-product-compliance
Lightning Source LLC
Chambersburg PA
CBHW020534270326
41927CB00006B/579